APACHE
LEGENDS & LORE
OF SOUTHERN NEW MEXICO

The Apaches gathered about the campfires within the teepees in winter to hear legends and lore of their past, their heroes' exploits and their ancient beginnings. *Photo by Mary Serna.*

APACHE LEGENDS & LORE
OF SOUTHERN NEW MEXICO

From the Sacred Mountain

LYNDA A. SÁNCHEZ

THE
History
PRESS

Published by The History Press
Charleston, SC 29403
www.historypress.net

Front cover: Sierra Blanca, *Mary Serna*; Apache Dancer, *Eric LeDuc*;
Percy Bigmouth, *author's collection.*
Back cover: Mescalero artist Ignatius Palmer's rendition of a Mescalero warrior, *author's
collection*; Teepee in winter, *Mary Serna.*

First published 2014
Second printing 2014

ISBN 978.1.54021.021.0

Library of Congress Cataloging-in-Publication Data

Sanchez, Lynda.
Apache legends and lore of southern New Mexico : from the sacred mountain / Lynda A.
Sanchez.
pages cm
Includes bibliographical references.
ISBN 978-1-62619-486-1
1. Apache Indians--New Mexico--Folklore. 2. Mescalero Indians--New Mexico--History.
3. Lipan Indians--History. 4. Mescalero Indians--New Mexico--Folklore. 5. Lipan Indians-
-Folklore. 6. Indian mythology. I. Bigmouth, Percy, 1891-1959. II. Title.
E99.A6S29 2014
979.004'9725--dc23
2014009997

I would like to dedicate this book to and express my gratitude to the family of Scout Bigmouth and especially Percy Bigmouth; the Apache people from Mescalero; the St. Joseph Apache Mission Restoration crew, along with Mary Serna and all those who love and appreciate the rich cultural mosaic represented by the legends and lore of the Apaches; and finally to all of those who choose to build bridges between and among cultures.

Author with Apache restoration crew (left to right): Tommy Spottedbird, Mary Serna, Martin Pizarro, author, Nikona Hosetosavit, Gilbert Garcia and Mary Mendez. *Courtesy Mary Serna.*

CONTENTS

CONTENTS

FOREWORD

No one is more passionate about preservation and history than author/historian Lynda Sánchez. Lynda has been a friend and sister preservationist for many years. She is an inspiration to many who work in the history and historic preservation fields.

Without this book, many of these ancient legends that are so precious to the Lipan and Mescalero Apache people would have been lost.

It is also exciting to see a man from our community recognized. It was Percy Bigmouth's deepest wish that the stories he shared with Eve Ball and wrote down for friends on his Big Chief tablets be saved and shared with future generations. Lynda has captured the heart of who Percy was and how much he loved his people and their history.

Enjoy these tales and remember well how things were not so long ago. Remember, too, how the elders used these stories to teach the children right from wrong in the Apache way.

Mary M. Serna
Director/Administrator
St. Joseph Apache Mission Restoration Project
Mescalero, New Mexico

MARY M. SERNA is the director/administrator of the St. Joseph Apache Mission Restoration Project at Mescalero, New Mexico. Her dedication and guidance have brought international attention to this sacred place. Mary's knowledge of regional history, her networking ability, her business management experience and her photographic talent have assisted in making this incredible renovation effort a success and one that will stand for yet another century.

Mary Serna, friend and sister preservationist.
Courtesy Mary Serna.

ACKNOWLEDGEMENTS

I am deeply grateful to my husband, James, for his patience, creative intuition and suggestions.

Thank you to Percy Bigmouth for the numerous reasons already listed throughout this book and for being the man who inspired completion of the manuscript.

Thanks also to my writing mentor, the late Eve Ball, author and oral historian, and for her collection of papers, letters and photographs that I now consider my own. I shall never forget the many lessons she has taught me.

Thank you to the late Gene Neyland Harris and her family and Mary Spencer Montgomery for their interest in preserving some of the legacy of the Apache legends and lore and the Percy Bigmouth story, which to date has only been available in fragments. Their generous sharing of letters, photographs and accounts given to them by Percy has become an important part of the story.

And thank you to the following friends and colleagues: Danna Henderson for the information and wonderful historic photographs of Old Scout Bigmouth and her father, artist Dan Kusianovich (chief administrative officer of Fort Stanton Tubercular Hospital for many years); Pam McArthur, *amiga especial*, for her concern, comments and suggestions; Ralph Grimes, Apache enthusiast and guitar player, who has shown a great interest in the Apaches and who wanted the first ten books from the first edition; Pete Lindsley, for his photographic expertise, patience and willingness to assist in any way I asked; Mr. Eugene Heathman, editor of the *Ruidoso Free Press*, for his interest and willingness to share photographs; Mr. Erik LeDuc, reporter for the *Ruidoso Free Press*, for his willingness to share photographs; Ms. Diane Stallings, reporter and friend; Mr. Phillip B. Gottfredson of Blackhawk Productions, LLC, for allowing me the use of one of his fine poems; artist Bob Boze Bell, executive editor of *True West Magazine*, for use of his illustration of Billy the Kid; historic photo expert and collector Robert (Bob) McCubbin for his interest and support; and Gary Stilwell for use of his illustration of Coyote, the trickster. At The History Press, I'd like to thank Jerry Roberts for his good cheer, creativity and steadfast guidance as my editor. The History Press design team's work throughout and especially on the cover is most appreciated, as is the editing work of Darcy Mahan.

A special thank-you to Mary Serna, restoration director/administrator at St. Joseph Apache Mission and Veterans' Memorial, friend, high-tech guru and the "go-to woman" for many aspects of tribal and St. Joseph Apache Mission history. Without her, I could not have completed the manuscript. Mary's photos are found throughout the book.

Thanks to Bev Strauser at the Dolan House for her support and the promise of my first "book signing," Carolyn Chrisman for her good care of the manuscript and author Chuck Usmar for his encouragement and photographic assistance. Thank you to Mescalero artist Mel Herrera and others who were intrigued by my project or who sent along information, ideas and thoughts: Judy Allen; Dan Aranda; Matt Barbour, manager of Jemez Historic Site, New Mexico; Ellen Bigrope; Mike Bilbo; Ron Booher; Bernd Brand; Bill Cavaliere; John Bloom; Dorothy Cave, biographer of Father Albert; Hugh Fox; Roger Harris; Bob Hart; K.J. Herman; Cheewa James; Tresa Jameson; Donna Knaff; Dr. Ron Lipinski; Ms. Rainee Mackewich; Gene Merrell; Karen Mills; Mary Ann Moorhouse; John Moses; Barbara Pruitt; Gwen Rogers; Dr. Deni Seymour; Van Shamblin; Lee Skinner; Aron Sánchez; Katherine Sánchez Meador; Dr. Robert Watt, of England; and numerous other friends and neighbors who asked, "When is your book going to be finished?" You all helped spur me on, and thus, I hope you enjoy *Apache Legends and Lore of Southern New Mexico*.

Photos or illustrations, unless otherwise noted, are courtesy of the Lynda Sánchez collection, which includes items from the Eve Ball materials and files, as well as other Fort Stanton and Apache history gathered by the author for almost four decades.

COMING FULL CIRCLE

*Our people's legends meant a lot to us as a people but now these young generation
don't see it that way…They never try to learn…too much of a White People's
way…But, I kept it in my sleeves.*
—Percy Bigmouth, 1949

Thus wrote Percy Bigmouth that cold November in 1949 to Gene
Neyland Harris, his friend of many years. Even at that time, Percy
understood what was happening to his own Apache culture and the old ways
he so revered. He was not pleased with the situation and longed to preserve
what he believed was important to Apache heritage. As a younger man, he
had learned through the work of ethnographers conducting research on the
Mescalero Reservation that the folklore and legends he and so many others
took for granted were sought-after pieces of the Apache history puzzle.
Percy worked for Morris Opler briefly and helped interpret a few of the
tales included in his ethno-history.

There were literally hundreds of such tales from separate bands within
the Apache tribe, such as Lipan, Jicarilla, Mescalero, Chiricahua and Warm
Springs. Percy did not appreciate at that time how important such information
was not only to the white man but especially for his own people, who were
fast becoming adapted to the dominant culture and thus forgetting their own
legacy. Years later, he realized that perhaps he, too, could help preserve some
of their beloved stories. However, with whom could he share the information,
would it really make a difference and what would be an appropriate venue?

Big Chief tablet cover.

Among the Apaches, there were (and still are) those who recognized the problems of losing their culture and language. Few, however, took the time to write down their colorful legends, history and lore, not even for family. That is what White Eyes (Anglos or white men) did. People often refer to holographic documents when they discuss writings such as Percy's. "Holographic" is a big word that simply means this material was written in Percy's own handwriting, a beautiful and prideful penmanship and, at the time, his only way of preserving what he believed was important information. This material was included in Big Chief tablets, popular in school settings nationwide.

The Apache view of history was also different in that they did not believe in preserving artifacts and other material items, nor did they much care about museums, although to some extent that view is changing. Unfortunately, much has already been lost or diluted over decades of constant exposure to a world that has become so high tech that one wonders if that other time even existed. Yes, the mists of time change everything.

Example of Percy's penmanship.

As the oral tradition of their society dictated, when an audience was at hand, the elders related tales of White Painted Woman, old trickster Coyote and his adventures and famous war leaders and raids. That had always been the traditional way to remember historical events. When people passed away, historically the Apaches burned all personal possessions—nothing was saved. That mindset prevailed for decades.

Nevertheless, in the Ruidoso Highlands of New Mexico, because of developing friendships over the years, Percy, a Mescalero-Lipan Apache, proceeded to record for his special friends what had been repeated to him around campfires as a youth or taught to him by his famous father, Old Scout Bigmouth, last of the living Apache Scouts. Old Bigmouth had lived to be over one hundred years of age, and he had seen incredible changes from the Bosque Redondo tragedy of the 1860s to the 1886 surrender of Geronimo in Skeleton Canyon, up until the time of his death in 1958. Percy continued to help interpret for his father and other elderly Apaches until his own passing on a dreary January 5, 1959.

Additionally, this book encompasses three other major players whom Percy knew and assisted in either interpreting, sharing of legends and history or whom he encountered as wide-eyed tourists visiting the Ruidoso Highlands: Eve Ball, Gene Neyland Harris and Mary Spencer Montgomery.

Eve Ball was born in 1890. Percy was born in 1891. Essentially, they were contemporaries from very different cultural backgrounds. Their paths crossed many times at Mescalero at the base of the Sacred Mountain (Sierra Blanca).

Then we have two other young women at that time (1930–50 New Mexico) who were representative of the numerous tourists who came to visit, enjoy and be inspired by the beauty and tranquility of this coveted haven. Their families maintained cabins in the area, and summers were delightful for them to be in the beautiful lands surrounding Sierra Blanca. Gene Neyland and Mary Spencer were two such individuals.

Eve Ball, well-known chronicler of the Apache and other area pioneers, became my writing mentor. I was fortunate to have accompanied her on visits to interview many of the aged Apaches, all sources of tribal history for Eve, as she researched her books and articles. She knew the Bigmouth family well. I also learned that Eve had befriended these Apaches in a much more personal manner than most people who only wished to "take" the Apaches' information for their own.

Times were tough on the reservation lands—even more so than the general poverty and struggles found throughout the nation after World War II. Although not everyone was affected, when needed, Eve often provided

Eve Ball being interviewed, circa 1968.

financial assistance or brought food, clothing or furniture to homes that had little. One year, a home had been devastated by fire, and Eve, in her quiet way, asked her friends to bring clothing, food, linens and furnishings to her own home. These were loaded in her 1950 Chevy coupe and dropped off at the Dutch Reformed Church. Another time, she brought boxes of food to St. Joseph Apache Mission to help the hungry.

Eve was quiet in demeanor and dedicated to writing. She is a recognized giant among oral historians and avid readers of our Southwestern history. I have, therefore, included relevant information about Eve and her invaluable work among the Apaches for those readers unfamiliar with her larger body of work. Recording the accounts of sixty-seven tribal elders over two decades was a daunting task. In other words, she did not just conduct a few interviews to lay claim to having interviewed Apaches. I soon discovered that Eve was welcomed into their homes and lives, and I was honored that they also brought me into their circle two decades later with sincere interest as to why yet another individual from the outside wanted to know about their intriguing history. Their integrity, humor and legends have taught me about life in ways I could never imagine. Some have become good friends.

We had both interviewed Mack Bigmouth, Percy's brother, for my manuscript on the Sierra Madre Apaches. I have since learned that Mack had also been honored during the August 1989 Mescalero Apache Heritage Day celebration, the first Heritage Day in Mescalero history. Ms. Evelyn Breuninger, a member of the tribal council, should be credited with organizing the successful ceremony. There were speeches, dances and a general celebratory atmosphere.

When she began the roll call of tribal elders, Mack Bigmouth, well into his nineties, was one of those who came forth. Though he used a cane and had difficulty walking, he continued on to the platform, turned and nodded a greeting to the audience. There were others too that day, but Mack was the oldest. It was good to have the elders honored, and no doubt everyone was pleased, including the Bigmouth family.

Another honoring of elders had occurred nine years before at the Golden Age Day of the Mescalero Apache Tribe, and Kate McGraw wrote in her article for *New Mexico Magazine* in January 1980:

Mack Bigmouth during a home visit relating family and tribal memories.

> *They have persevered, these old ones, in the faces of tragedy and want and happiness and progress. They have come through...and their wisdom and courage is valued. That was evident in the speeches of the middle-aged Apaches who stood in public that day to honor them...the most moving speeches on this...day were not those made by the tribal leaders...They were the halting testimonials about individual elders from members of their own families.*
>
> *Richard Magoosh [a Lipan] was praised by his daughter as a man who "worked endlessly to put food on the table during the hard times and still saw to it that we had a little candy"...*
>
> *There was a lesson evident that day; to stop and remember just how much those who have walked these paths before us have helped our way.*

However, forty years before these events, another tribal elder, Percy Bigmouth, was in despair because it appeared to him that the old ways were rapidly being forgotten. He did not foresee events such as the two noted above or that others would be interested in his people's accounts of history and myths. He simply saw the collective knowledge of the past slipping away.

The majority of Percy's hand-written letters and legends came to me after I had written an article about Eve Ball for *New Mexico Magazine* in April 1981. Dr. Jackson Harris, originally from Albuquerque, was trying to find someone who would understand the material and possibly publish some of the unique letters and Apache folklore from the era of the 1940s. Mailed to his wife, then Martha Gene Neyland, there were Big Chief tablets full of legends, coyote tales and other stories along with some poignant letters and four photographs. I talked to Eve, and we were both interested in working on fleshing out such a manuscript—especially after she found out Percy Bigmouth was the source of the materials. The story of the Bigmouths was one that had not fully been told. Perhaps this material would be a good venue. I obtained more photographs and information from Eve, and we were excited about the pending manuscript.

This was, of course, the pre-computer era. However, time and events were not on our side. Sadly, my mentor and friend passed on to the land beyond the shining mountains in 1984.

I was devastated. I was also finishing school and had my full-time teaching job and a ranch to help run. The material languished.

Fast-forward about three decades, and the computer age had arrived. I am now "retired," and my journey has led me to the rugged Sierra Madre of Mexico, which was always a safe haven for Apaches during the war years. Additional travels throughout the Southwestern United States have added to my knowledge, and I have had the privilege of teaching many students of Apache heritage both at the college and high school levels from Mescalero. I have also had the privilege of working with Mary Serna at the St. Joseph Apache Mission in Mescalero on its unique restoration project.

Readers should also understand that Apaches of old passed on verbatim events, messages or folklore by repetition. Their memories were excellent. Survival often depended on getting it right the first time. Therefore, in editing, I have kept to a minimum the repetition yet allowed the unusual vernacular, punctuation and style to prevail. As you read, try to conjure up the sound and rhythm of these words and their unusual phrasing.

It has become my greatest hope that the reader will come to appreciate the Apache and their love of land and family and to realize that they are much like we are in our best moments, whether in our angry and sad days or laughing out loud with the comical antics of Coyote or Raven.

There are several heretofore unpublished photos that are also part of the legacy left by Percy. Gene Neyland Harris and Mary Spencer Montgomery, both Percy's cherished friends, sent along letters to the author and photos from those years. I have since gathered numerous other images and historic photos from my own collection or through various colleagues who have been incredibly generous and whose names are in the acknowledgements of this book.

A beginning chapter about general tribal history and traditions has been added encompassing the varied backgrounds of the Apache people. Separate chapters about Percy and his father are included, and the final chapters yield many of the legends, favorite lore and myths related mostly by Percy to his friends over time. The accounts will be grouped according to theme with explanations and historical background to assist the reader in understanding the Apache way.

After three decades, the phone call to officially complete the manuscript came as I was informed by editor Jerry Roberts of The History Press that my contract was in the mail. It was indeed time to complete the circle that encompasses the outreach of Percy Bigmouth and his wish to preserve some of the hundreds of legends and folklore of the Mescalero/Lipan Apaches that were part of his world and will surely enrich our own. It is my wish that the desire of the Harris family, Mary Montgomery, Eve Ball and many others to share Percy Bigmouth's story in his own phrasing and words and to finish construction of that bridge between and among cultures will at last be completed.

Percy would be pleased to know that he helped protect examples of the ancient humor, social mores and values of the people who continue to live in the shadow of the Sacred Mountain so honored by the Apaches.

Part 1

IN THE SHADOW OF THE SACRED MOUNTAIN

Chapter 1

HISTORY AND TRADITIONS
OF THE APACHE

Every morning I walk to the tent of the mountain.
I stand secure.
I am in peace.
The wind comes.
There the breath of the mountain telling me the path to take.

I am gone and am going to the mountain so that I may see the lightening break the
sky in two
and rain come to heal it up again.
I come to the place where I have stepped before.
The wind blows my steps away in the dust.
The steps of all who walk here go with the wind and walk with the sky...
—Phillip B. Gottfredson, Blackhawk Productions, LLC

The Sacred Mountain

Within the Apache homeland lie four sacred mountains: Sierra Blanca, Guadalupe Mountains, Three Sisters Mountain and Oscura Mountain Peak. These four mountains represent the direction of everyday life for the residents of Mescalero. However, for the Mescaleros, one mountain is supreme, and that is Sierra Blanca, or White Mountain, and its surrounding sacred peaks. Only the tribal elders know to which peak certain attributes can be credited or which is more sacred for medicine and special power. For this book, we shall simply refer to them all as the "White Mountain."

Grandparents would often speak of the place called White Mountain. It was there that the creator (*Ussen*) gave the Apaches life. It was on White Mountain that White Painted Woman gave birth to two sons. They were born during a rainstorm when thunder and lightning ripped through the heavens. When they grew to be men, the two sons, Child of the Water and Killer of Enemies, rose up and killed the monsters of the earth. Then came peace, and all human beings were saved.

That is the short version. Percy's account is far more detailed and will fill in numerous details regarding the origin of the Apaches.

The Mescaleros are very fortunate to have a reservation in the heart of their traditional territory instead of the vast desert lands or unproductive country "given" to other bands of Apaches or Indian tribes in general. Their sacred mountain, Sierra Blanca, plays a significant role in Mescalero ceremonial and traditional practices. It is used as holy ground for ceremonies, seeking visions and collecting medicinal herbs, and it is said to be the origin of more than one mountain spirit dance group.

Sierra Blanca also provided the same bounty for the ancient Jornada Mogollon people and the desert culture inhabitants who preceded them five to ten thousand years ago.

The many moods and shadows of the Sacred Mountain entice the viewer to meet the challenge of the rugged 12,003-foot peak towering

Sierra Blanca, the Sacred Mountain. *Photo by Pete Lindsley.*

above everything else for hundreds of miles. The whispers of the ancients, the drums, the chants and the dances of the mountain spirits will also continue forever because even today, special ceremonies of the Apache prevail and are conducted annually, much as they were when the Apache were a free people.

Providing water and wildlife, the mountain was like a great fortress or refuge when the Apaches were pursued by the white man and other enemies. It was a training ground for Apache boys as they came of age. They looked to the Sacred Mountain to begin their preparations as warriors. Fasting and praying, they would sometimes have visions or their spirit animals would make an appearance and become part of the young man's life from that point on. Many also carried a small leather medicine bag along with *hoddentin* (sacred pollen) and other talismans that had meaning in their lives.

Following Red-Tailed Hawk

The haunting cry of a red-tailed hawk as it soars over lands dominated by the Sacred Mountain reminds us that the territory over which this magnificent hawk flies today has changed little through the centuries. True, there are more people, towns and villages appearing along the rivers and once well-traveled trails, but the lands of the Mescalero country remain much the same. The hawk's bird's-eye view would reveal an ancient land and a culturally rich New Mexico dependent on its natural and cultural heritage. It is an adventure in itself to follow along the trail of the red-tailed hawk, a creature some consider a "spirit animal." In following the hawk, one learns about the Apache

Red-tailed hawk.

who considered this bountiful yet harsh land their home long before the arrival of the Spanish and Anglo pioneers. The Mescalero, Chiricahua and a few Lipan still live here and are part of the colorful mosaic of people inhabiting the region.

For centuries, populations ebbed and flowed within this territory of abundant harvests and devastating drought. Because of this "feast or famine" situation, the Apaches relied less on agricultural activities and more on hunting, raiding, trading and gathering. It worked very well for centuries until the final clash with the White Eyes.

At about the same time that the sedentary culture of the Jornada Mogollon people was disappearing, a new wave of nomads made their way into the greater Southwest, eventually becoming a significant force of conflict within the Native American community and with the newer European settlers. The Apaches had traditionally raided Pueblo villages for women and food supplies and Mexican and American settlements for horses and ammunition and other goods they could not obtain from the Pueblos. They raided deep into Mexico and as far north as Colorado.

Although there were many bands of Apaches scattered throughout the Southwest, those who dominated the lands around Sierra Blanca were the Mescalero. Named by the Spanish for their gathering of the mescal plant, they became known as Mescaleros. They were divided into two groups. A Plains-like culture raided and lived in Texas, especially in the Fort Davis, Big Bend and Guadalupe Mountain areas, while the Sierra Blancas dominated the mountain country.

The Bountiful Land

Most people driving through the area today don't realize they are passing through an amazing, still wild and bountiful country. A southwestern pantry of edible plants and creatures used by the Native Americans of all tribes both prehistorically and into the modern era provided a well-balanced, high-fiber and delicious repertoire. Later, when the European newcomers invaded, they also learned and made use of *la cocina del Apache*, the Apache kitchen.

Primary vegetable products used for food by the Apaches and their neighbors were numerous. Mescal and yucca were of major importance. There are many varieties of yucca. The Spanish bayonet plant produced fruit that resembles bananas and is known as "Indian bananas." The native peoples called this *oosa* and ate it either raw or roasted in hot ashes.

Datil, sotol, piñon (for nuts, firewood and incense for ceremonies), mesquite (for medicinal purpose, the rich seeds for flour and wood for fire) and dozens of roots, tubers and berries, along with pine nuts and acorns, were eaten raw, roasted or ground into flour. Mesquite beans were cooked with meat. Sometimes tasty dumplings were made of mesquite or acorn flour.

Los Mescaleros (The Mescal Gatherers)

Honey and mescal were two favorite sweets. To gather the honey from beehives, men would place a hide or canvas at the bottom of a tree or ledge. Then they would shoot arrows at the beehive until it fell onto the buckskin. Sometimes they also used smoke to create chaos in the bee colony, often hidden inside a hollow tree or cave. To gather the sweet delicacy was an exciting moment in their lives as it was so rare. Percy often described their fingers covered with the sweet *miel* (honey) and what a feast they had. They also left part of the honeycomb so that the bees would survive during the winter months. Bees ate the honey to survive until spring came once again to the land.

Mescal, which grew at higher elevations, was the staple food of the Mescaleros and has a sweet, smoky flavor. Apaches probably learned how to harvest the mescal or century (agave) plant from indigenous peoples to the south in Mexico. The men and boys would often help the women remove the heads (*piñas*, so called because of their resemblance to pineapples) or crowns of the plant (think of a large artichoke in the ground). After digging a long pit four to five feet deep, they lined it with rocks. A fire using mesquite wood produced good coals. Shoveling the glowing coals over the rock, they added layers of green, water-soaked grass. The crowns and long leaves of the mescal were put in upright with the tips being visible from the tamped earth. These would later be pulled out for testing the readiness of the mescal. The mescal heads were covered with more wet grass and canvas bags and about two feet of dirt. Sometimes steam would be visible, and the boys would immediately add more dirt to keep the heat inside the pit. It was a time-consuming process.

The mescal pits were blessed by medicine men, and after three days of cooking slowly, at long last when the dirt, stones and grass were removed and the smoky crowns were taken out of the large pits, the peoples' hearts sang of work well done.

Piñas or cabbage-like heads of mescal would be covered with a sweet, sticky coating, and everyone looked with anticipation as the women sliced them and handed around the prize. The remainder would be placed in the sun to dry and later stored in various caches for the winter, just like the dried beef and venison jerky.

During the last part of the military campaign to destroy the Apaches, one group of soldiers was said to have destroyed hundreds—perhaps thousands—of pounds of both jerky and mescal as they swept down into just one *ranchería*. One can imagine what a blow that was to the Apaches after their days, maybe even weeks, of work, and it became yet another reason to hide or cache their food supplies, along with weapons, bolts of calico and other important survival items.

There are large pits found throughout the Apaches' homeland, and once you know how to recognize them it is amazing how many have been dated back centuries. The people returned annually to their favorite harvesting areas. They also gathered the prickly pear's fleshy pads and fruit. Once the sharp spines were removed, the prickly pear pads were eaten and often used as a poultice for wounds. Buds of the *cholla* cactus could be dried or used in stews and are an excellent source of calcium.

The ocotillo is high in protein, and its seeds, flowers and stalks can be used as a medicinal tea for pain and swelling or cough. Of course, the Apache had no understanding about calcium or protein content, yet the land provided a well-balanced and harmonious bounty.

Other unique plants include: *Chuchupate* (wild angelica root) found in the higher elevations on Sierra Blanca and used as an herbal medicine for intestinal upset, chest colds and cough and greasewood (creosote), which was very strong and pungent after a rain in the lowlands and had medical value in its leaves ground into a powder with primary use as an antiseptic. The Four Wing salt bush had several uses for both its green leaves and seeds that could be ground into flour or cooked with stew.

The tough and wide-ranging juniper tree, in addition to providing firewood, found the native folk using its berries for spicing up stews or brewing it as a tea for cough.

Fruit of the *datil* was nearly as important for subsistence as mescal. Like mescal, its storage properties were excellent. Although this shrub had a wide distribution depending on rain, the fruit produced was subject to moisture. The tender flowers were used as one would a fresh fruit, and the

Desert Moon

Above: Yucca, "Buffalo of the Plant World." *Illustration by Gary Stilwell.*

Right: Apache basket maker utilizing yucca, sotol and bear grass in construction.

"Baskets are the Apache woman's poetry," said one old warrior.

plant in general, like the yucca and *sotol*, was valued for other purposes. The main roots were used for soap and shampoo, the small red side roots for basket work and the leaves for twine and rope. Paintbrushes made of yucca leaves were produced especially by the Pueblos for painting of designs on ceramics. (These ceramics were sometimes traded or raided from Pueblo villages by the nomadic Apaches.) In fact, the yucca plant is often referred to as the "buffalo" of the plant world because of its many uses. Bats, moths, hummingbirds and bees all helped cross-pollinate these plants and played a major role in keeping the desert eco-system in balance.

Other gifts from *Ussen* were grass seeds, wild potatoes, onions, okra, walnuts from the elegant native black walnut trees growing along the rivers, strawberries, wild blackberries, elderberries, sumac berries, grapes and plums. Both the walnut and mesquite trees were also messengers of winter's end. These trees proved to be good weather barometers, as their leaves come out only when frost is gone from the earth. They are rarely wrong.

Cochineal and Hoddentin

Another of the gifts from nature to all Native Americans, including the Apaches, was actually a parasite, living on its host plant the prickly pear. The fiery crimson or scarlet color (much like that of the fruit of the same plant) of the cochineal insect, when dried and ground into powder, provided a beautiful and long-lasting color that many Native American cultures appreciated and some groups highly valued as a trade item. Boiled in water with urine and the leaf of the sycamore, the colors produced were widely sought after by Spaniards and Indians alike. It was native to the New World and used extensively by the Aztec, Maya and other tribes of Mexico and the Southwest.

Next to gold and silver, cochineal powder became the most important export to Spain when the Spaniards came into the New World as conquerors for the "glory of God and the King of Spain." The conquistadors found huge leather bags of the valuable dye in storage vaults along with the riches of empires. Other minerals, clay and insects were ground and used for paint as well. Several pictographs indicate crimson colors were sometimes utilized and could have come from cochineal powder. Faded after decades or centuries, they are still visible

Prickly pear, host plant for cochineal. *Photo by James Sánchez.*

in isolated shelters or caves throughout the New Mexico and Arizona landscape. These would also include Apache pictographs.

Hoddentin, pollen of the tule (wild rush or cattail), was carried by warriors on every expedition as a protection. A small sack of it was given to children born into the tribe. It was used in their prayers to the sun, the moon and the stars. It was believed that this *hoddentin* was once scattered along the face of the heavens and thus formed the Milky Way. It was used to a very great extent in all the Apaches' ceremonials and their medicine man's blessings. Even in contemporary Catholic or Protestant churches, one observes the medicine man blessing the people or those involved in a baptism or other event. Attendees show the mark of the pollen on their faces. In some areas, this has been replaced by corn pollen, but *hoddentin* is preferred by the Apaches.

Edible parts of the cattail include the starchy roots, inner parts of the young shoots and pollen. The flour made from the *tule* is also very nutritious and was used in many recipes. The spikes could be cooked and eaten like corn on the cob, and pollen was added in equal parts to flour or meal.

The Hunter's Bounty

Animals of greatest significance for the Mescalero larder included deer, elk, antelope and bison. Rabbits were hunted occasionally and might become important in periods of drought. A number of other animals were hunted for use of their skins and feathers or for food in desperate times. Lion, mountain sheep, badger, *javelina* or peccary, bobcat, wolf, coyote, fox and birds like turkey, quail, hawks and eagles were also included in the diversity of the Apache homeland. Bears and owls were feared and avoided. Fish and other water animals were not used until contact with Europeans. They would not eat animals that ate snakes, and a great fear of snakes has always been prevalent among the Apaches. (I experienced this many times in classroom settings while teaching Southwestern history. Any mention of snakes or an appearance of one in a show-and-tell situation would upset my Apache students.) Mule and horsemeat were also enjoyed, and as beef became available, the Apache developed a taste for that as well.

Percy described how they cut and dried deer or beef for making jerky in his family. "Old Dad" taught them how to properly slice and jerk (dry) the meat. He also taught them the traditional way of hunting the deer and described old-timers using a mask and hide to stalk the deer. One had to hunt carefully and avoid eating strong foods such as onion the day before because the deer could pick up on this strong smell. The men covered themselves from head to foot while they moved in slowly among the deer herd. Percy portrayed how one old man decided to play a joke but instead got wounded himself when the hunters thought he was a deer. "You make good deer!" they shouted, and then they all laughed.[1]

Other Gifts from Ussen

Bark was used for shelters, as were the branches of conifers. Soft grass became diapers. Peyote and wild tobacco rolled in oak leaves were used for smoking on occasion. Apaches did not use pipes unless they had ties with the Plains peoples. The yellow, round fruit of the Datura plant was used to help curdle milk and, if eaten, was a hallucinogen.

Salt, various wood and sand stones for *manos* (hand grinder) for grinding and other implements all added to the Mescalero pantry of goods. It must also be remembered that these foodstuffs and other items, like salt, were found only in specific places and on a seasonal basis. This meant that the Mescalero and Lipan, like other groups, subsisted by moving from one location to another. Each band ordinarily following an annual cycle would sometimes overlap with that of another. This usually was not a problem, and often they met, camped together and perhaps even chose partners from another group, thus keeping the bloodlines open and not limited. Sometimes they danced and celebrated and then moved on to other favorite places. It was an independent and free lifestyle.

Housing was designed to fit their environment. The Kiowa-Apaches, Jicarillas, Lipans and some Mescaleros lived in teepees on the edge of the Plains and carried that tradition into the mountain country. Some Apaches made teepees from wooden poles covered with bison hide. Teepees offered temporary, portable housing as the people followed bison herds across the plains.

Other Apache bands, especially those from Arizona, lived in *wickiups*, round huts made of brush with scooped-out earthen floors. The *wickiups'* outer covering changed with the weather. In summertime, people draped leafy branches over the dwellings to provide shade and ventilation. In winter, they used tanned animal hides for insulation or heavy canvas once that had been introduced to them by the military. They often built larger *wickiups*

A rare photo of both teepees and *wickiups* at Mescalero, circa 1900.

with holes in the center so that smoke from cooking fires could escape. Both teepees and *wickiups* were ideal housing for hunters and gatherers who moved as the winds across their lands as the seasons changed. Both styles were used at Mescalero. Dogs transported many items as they pulled the *travois*. However, once the horse became part of their lifestyle, it was much easier to move heavy supplies and to ride in grand style compared to the times when they had to walk to every campsite.

White Men Arrive

From the time of the first Europeans (the Spanish conquistadors) entering the Southwest through the era of Spanish control, Mexican independence and Anglo pioneers flooding into their homeland, it is understandable that hostilities would emerge with the Native Americans who inhabited the land. Fierce battles would be fought, and many lives would be lost. With each loss, an encyclopedia of cultural information was destroyed. From 1540 until 1886, the area was a maelstrom of conflict. Comanches also began to crowd the Mescalero and

Lipan as each group vied for new territory. The Lipan, Mescalero and just about every other Native American group were also victims of the Spaniards' insatiable desire to capture slaves for the rich *hacendados* (land owners) or to work their fields and mines. It got so bad in some instances that even the early priests became angered by these actions, and though some tried to prevent the slave raids, they could not stop them. Others criticized the church, insisting that it was part of the problem as it, too, needed laborers and servants. We will never know how many Apaches and other tribal people were sold into slavery or sent to Cuba, the Yucatan, Mexico City and points in between.

In 1848, New Mexico and much of the Southwest and California were ceded to the United States via the Treaty of Guadalupe Hidalgo. By the early 1850s, Hispanic families, mostly sheepherders and small agriculturalists, began moving into *placitas,* or villages, along the river valleys of southern New Mexico. *Torreons,* or two-story towers, became defensive shelters during times of attacks. (An excellent example of a *torreon* can be seen in historic Lincoln.) Cultural clashes occurred, yet more settlers continued to arrive, thus providing a recipe for disaster.

Fort Stanton was established in 1855 to prevent further conflict. That did not mean tensions had ended, but it was the beginning of a slow, steady stranglehold on the lands within its reach. Kit Carson was the first to receive major orders detailing deliberate destruction of the Mescalero Apaches.

Stunning orders came from General James Carleton, who, in his absolute desire to destroy the Mescaleros, had virtually no mercy or concern. Carleton ordered Kit Carson, in an infamous 1862 letter, to see that "there is to be no council held with the Indians, nor any talks. The men are to

Kit Carson.

Apaches at Fort Stanton, circa 1875. Note the extreme poverty and traumatized appearance of each person.

be slain whenever and wherever they can be found. The women and children may be taken prisoners...I trust that these...demonstrations will give those Indians a wholesome lesson." The women and children were to be held at Fort Stanton until Carson received other instructions.

Those instructions were not long in coming. By December 1862, Cadette, along with several other leaders, sued for peace, and the tragedy known as the Bosque Redondo was about to begin. Thousands of Navajos and about 475 Mescaleros were forced to live together along the Pecos River near Fort Sumner, far from the beloved Sacred Mountain. It was a black episode in the history of native peoples in New Mexico.

By 1866, observers agreed this holding area was a disaster. Carleton was relieved of his command, and New Mexico breathed a sigh of relief. Before the military returned the Navajo to their traditional lands in 1868, most of the Mescaleros had already disappeared into their mountain hideouts, vowing never again to be taken to such a terrible place. Shortly afterward, even military officials recognized their miserable failure, and the Bosque Redondo "experiment" was abandoned.

Eventually, a reservation was established in 1873, allowing the Mescalero to return to the heart of their homeland, with Sierra Blanca included as part of the reservation. However, discord continued and became a way of life measured in sporadic raids on villages and retaliatory attacks by Anglo farmers and the military. There was never enough food, and other supplies were severely rationed. Corruption was rampant. Many Mescaleros stayed hidden for years in the mountains rather than come into the newly formed reservation. The experience of Bosque Redondo remained fresh in their memories.

They were blamed for theft or crimes committed, yet the White Man was rarely—if ever—punished for stealing their horses, raiding their *rancherías* or selling bootleg whiskey. There was no trust. There was no bridge. There was little hope.

On the periphery were valiant warriors or leaders like Victorio, Geronimo, Santana and others who were suspicious of anything promised by the White Eyes. A few, like Dr. Paul Blazer and family, were trusted, but they were the exceptions. Blazer's Mill (*La Maquina*) between Tularosa and Mescalero was a major landmark and source of labor and supplies. The Blazer family, from the beginning, had integrated into the daily lives of the Mescalero. Their descendants today play major roles in tribal policy.

Victorio, a Warm Springs (Chihenne) Apache, often came into the reservation lands with his people for rest, for supplies and perhaps with some desire to live as they once had. But that was an ill-fated dream for the followers of Victorio. Before his final flight from Mescalero, Victorio shook hands with Dr. Blazer and noted with regret that they would never again be confined to the boundaries created for Apaches by white men when he said, "From now on it will be war…war to the death. There is no other way." Victorio died in Mexico a short time later, and many of his people were captured and sold into slavery. A few hid in the Sierra Madre and raided periodically into the Southwestern United States under the leadership of old Nana.

Unfortunately, more bridges needed to be created, but during those times, as is so often the situation, the peaceful and innocent suffered for the actions

The commissary area at Bosque Redondo, a bleak and sad place. *Courtesy Matt Barbour.*

of the more warlike Mescaleros. General (Edward) Hatch ordered the entire Mescalero tribe disarmed and sent troops to the agency for that purpose. They killed many, including "one helpless group [that] was slaughtered when camped near the agency to draw rations."[2] This cycle of violence confused the Sierra Blanca Mescalero, so they continued hiding in the mountains. It was, no doubt, a wise decision for their survival.

Another of the more intriguing characters of the Apache Wars was James Kaywaykla, who, like Victorio, was a Warm Springs Apache. However, his life was intertwined with the Mescaleros by relatives, friends and lifestyle, especially after the Mescaleros accepted the last of the Chiricahua POWs as residents of their reservation in 1913. Kaywaykla also decided to return to Mescalero from Oklahoma.

During many interviews with Eve Ball, he stressed, "Until I was about ten years old, I did not know that people died except by violence. That is

Above: Buffalo Soldier drill. Encounters with Buffalo Soldiers and Apaches were constant and violent. *Courtesy Ernestine Chesser Williams.*

Left: James Kaywaykla knew only violence and raiding as his first childhood memories.

because I am an Apache...whose first vivid memories are of being driven from our homeland."[3]

Kaywaykla passed on to the "Happy Place" of the Apache in 1963, but not before he helped author Eve Ball garner a better understanding of what life was like for his family and his people. He had, as a child, experienced what so many had: an early life of betrayal and tragedy. He had survived, however, and for that we must all be grateful for we now have much of his story, his side of events, in written form that can be passed on to all who have an interest in the regional history of the Apaches. Kaywaykla, like Percy, had much to share.

Much later, after the Apache Wars ended in 1886, the Mescalero also generously opened their reservation to the Lipan. In 1903, a small group of starving Lipan Apaches were rescued from a corral-like pen where they were being kept in Chihuahua. They had been prisoners for a long time and, starving and wretched, had become broken human beings. Some of them were escaped slaves. They had been living hand to mouth but were finally rescued and brought to Mescalero. A few others struggled to find homes in Texas and elsewhere in New Mexico, but most ended up at Mescalero.

The Chiricahua Apache POWs who needed a place to come back to after their twenty-seven years of imprisonment (1886–1913) in Florida, Alabama and Fort Sill, Oklahoma, arrived in the shadow of the Sacred Mountain and set up their homes at White Tail. Over the years, intermarriage between different bands became the norm, and each group that was granted a place became united and recognized as Mescalero Apache. Of course, the genealogy of each individual remained an important part of most families. Scout Bigmouth and his family also found a safe haven at Mescalero.

Father Albert's Vision

During this time of change, another strong character emerged. He was a white man who bore the burden of righting many wrongs. A gentle giant of a man, revered by both sides and by young and old, Apache, Hispanic and Anglo, Father Albert Braun, long an advocate for the Apaches, came to Mescalero as a very young priest in 1916. He, too, met the survivors of the Apache Wars, including Scout Bigmouth and his family. The old Apache's long life ultimately reached beyond the century mark. However, at the turn

Left: Father Albert Braun receiving the Silver Star from General Wainwright. He and Eve Ball became close confidants. *Courtesy St. Joseph Apache Mission.*

Below: St. Joseph Apache Mission. *Photo by Mary Serna.*

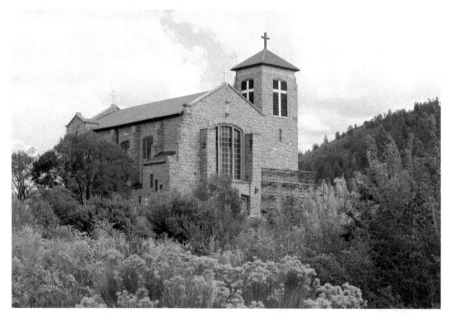

of the century, Scout Bigmouth was still rearing a family of four boys. Father Albert enjoyed the company of Scout Bigmouth, along with numerous others, and began to learn their side of history. He concluded in his foreword to *In the Days of Victorio*:

> Much has been written by the White Man about the Apache… Accounts…written as military reports by young officers ambitious for promotion; or reports were… compiled by Indian agents; by contemporary newspapers whose owners depended upon advertising paid for by merchants who lived by selling supplies to the reservations, by pioneers who entered the country occupied and claimed by the Apaches…Some were written by men who wanted to take over Apache country…seeking the support of public opinion, these intruders often picture the Apaches…as a people who should be driven from the mountains of the Southwest.[4]

Partial truths are really lies, and soon Father Albert and others began to flesh out the entire culture and history of the Apache people. There were a few far-sighted tribal elders who described the early days and who entrusted some white people with their folklore, religious beliefs and their sides of events. Archaeological

St. Joseph Apache Mission

Father Albert's vision when he came back from France after World War I and later from World War II, where he was a survivor of Corregidor and incarcerated as a POW along with the men of the dreaded Bataan Death March, was to create a mission to serve his people at Mescalero. While a POW, he had suffered cruelty beyond measure in beatings and starvation tactics. As a tall man of about 200 pounds, he had wasted away to 115 by the end of the war, enduring malaria, dysentery and other horrible jungle diseases. After more than three years, he, along with the other POWs, was liberated on August 29, 1945.

From humble beginnings after World War I to the now grand monument dedicated to all veterans of all wars, St. Joseph Mission was referred to by some as an "impossible dream translated into soaring stone." Through years of blood, sweat and many tears, Father Albert's vision came to fruition. Anyone who visits or who has been involved with the ongoing restoration work at the mission today acknowledges that it changes their lives forever. Percy Bigmouth and his family were part of that

Father Albert as a chaplain returning from World War II with his people. *Courtesy St. Joseph Apache Mission.*

Winter at St. Joseph Apache Mission. The mission has since become a veterans' memorial for all veterans. *Photo by Mary Serna.*

records and other ethnographic accounts filled in additional pieces of the puzzle.

Percy Bigmouth and family members from both the Lipan and Mescalero sides of the family turned to Father Albert and became members of the parish. Percy was confirmed there on June 23, 1918, long before this magnificent building was finished.

Entering the Twenty-First Century

World Wars I and II created numerous changes on the reservation, as elsewhere in the United States. Educational opportunities, off-reservation employment, boarding schools and utilization of their ancestral resources also transformed tribal life. Wounds from the Apache Wars were beginning to heal, and understanding of cultural differences began to occur.

The Apache developed a cattle industry and conducted timber sales. One of the best forest firefighting units anywhere—the Red Hats—continue that proud tradition among their young men and women. Eco-tourism seemed to be a viable way to enhance tribal funds, but numerous Apaches believed the mountain was sacred and should not be accessible to non-

history as well. Helping Father Albert succeed was part of their dream too.

The restoration crew has worked for more than a decade not just to restore this magnificent church, stone by stone, but also to train young people in a trade that builds self-esteem and knowledge of their heritage. The project provides a cornerstone and a bridge to cultural gaps as both Mescaleros and their Anglo and Hispanic neighbors work side by side in this current preservation effort. The restoration team and all participants are reaching out to others, and this is so typical of their attitude since we all have, indeed, a common battle to preserve our past. Dr. Blazer, Santana, Victorio, Scout Bigmouth, Percy Bigmouth, Eve Ball, Gene Neyland Harris and so many others long gone would be pleased. Building bridges is no easy task, but St. Joseph Apache Mission is one example that it can be achieved.

Father Albert would certainly agree that by preserving this veterans' memorial and National Landmark, the Mescaleros are working through a process "that strives to honor their ancestors, empower their contemporaries and inspire their children."

Percy Bigmouth, fourth from left, at Mescalero during a special celebration. *Courtesy St. Joseph Apache Mission.*

Coming-of-age or puberty ceremonials, circa 1920s.

tribal members. How does one protect the spiritual needs of the tribe yet allow guided hunts, hiking and fishing? While some employment has been created, old traditions held fast, and many of the younger folks refused to work on any project that would physically scar or change the mountain.[5]

Over several years, compromise has taken hold, and today, for example, during the Fourth of July, the tribe opens its reservation to rodeo, a popular sport among many tribes and tourists alike. Tribe members also allow the public to view their puberty ceremonials and other celebrations. The puberty ceremony is one of the most vivid and beautiful coming-of-age celebrations anywhere in the world. The young girls represent White Painted Woman, mother of Child of the Water and Killer of Enemies. She provides the moral compass for the girls. Relatives participate in preparations such as sewing buckskin dresses, cooking huge amounts of food, purchasing gifts and other family-oriented projects for many months prior to the actual event. Lasting four days, it is a joyous time for everyone.

Today, the tribe owns a ski resort and is in the process of discussing a land swap with the United States Forest Service. It also owns a casino and the Inn of the Mountain Gods. The Mescaleros have created a tribal historic preservation office whose responsibility is "to maintain and research ties with the past." Professional archaeologists are on staff, and a tribal cultural center exhibits intriguing artifacts from their past, although much is still lacking in terms of telling the total history of the Apache through exhibits and archiving their storied past.

The reservation lands occupy over 475,000 acres, and there are more than five thousand tribal members in residence. A few live off the reservation in nearby communities, but most of them are living on the reservation.

Thus, as the beginning years of the twenty-first century are upon us, we observe a vibrant people, the Mescalero (and all those who have been absorbed into the tribe), who are prosperous and eager to face the future on their own lands and on their own terms with their sovereign government in place with talented and powerful leaders. Ideally, wise tribal elders understand that their traditions must continue, their language must be maintained and that pride of culture can continue only with a strong corps of adept and skillful individuals who will lead them into the future. And dedicated individuals like Percy Bigmouth, his father and others who have helped lay the cornerstones for that future must surely be smiling down on the vast lands of the Mescalero.

Chapter 2

THE LEGACY OF SCOUT BIGMOUTH (1855?–1958)

We were cold, hungry and miserable. Above all, we were homesick for our country and our freedom...What man can bear to hear his child crying for food and do nothing?
—*Scout Bigmouth*

And we Mescaleros are horse Indians. We don't like to walk.
—*Scout Bigmouth*

In late December 1958, the elderly Scout Bigmouth passed on to the "Happy Place," the land of *Ussen*, where the Apache believed beautiful, tall pines and lush meadows with pure water in tiny streams watered the land and the wild creatures. The dominant Sacred Mountain, Sierra Blanca, also cast its shadow over all who inhabited the hills and valleys beneath. His passing was mourned by many.

In isolated places like Gadsden, Alabama, someone had included his simple obituary on December 2, 1958, in the *Gadsden Times*, so far away from Mescalero. (Mt. Vernon Barracks in Alabama was one of the places the Apache POWs were imprisoned for several years.)

*Last Apache (*sic *Scout) Dies at 108*
Alamogordo New Mexico, AP, describes briefly the death of Scout Bigmouth. Bigmouth, famous as the last of the Apache Scouts was buried at Mescalero, NM Monday. He died Friday at the age of 108. Bigmouth, the only name he ever had, served as a Scout for the U.S. Cavalry during

Scout Bigmouth with service medal, 1938. *Photo by Dan Kusianovich, Fort Stanton, courtesy Danna Kusianovich Henderson.*

the Indian Wars. He had lived at Mescalero for 95 years and had served as reservation peace officer.

Such a short commentary on a long, varied, difficult yet blessed life did not begin to cover what Scout Bigmouth encountered in his more than one hundred years at the base of the Sacred Mountain, nor did it do him justice in terms of the legacy he left behind.

Before his passing, Scout Bigmouth described the plight of the captive Apaches, saying:

They put men and women to work digging ditches and digging up ground with shovels to plant corn. And once a week the soldiers gave us enough food to last perhaps two days. We were not farmers—we were fighters and hunters! Above all, we were free people; and now we were imprisoned within picket lines and made into slaves. The Apache does not mind work, but he does not like slavery. We were cold, hungry and miserable. Above all, we were homesick for our country and our freedom.

These and other heart-rending revelations continued to pour forth from the heart of the ancient Apache known as "Old Dad," or Scout Bigmouth, the last living scout of the Apache Wars.

The tribal elder knew no English, but his son and caregiver, Percy, accompanied Eve Ball on several occasions to interview his father. Eve was continually struck by the suffering and loss experienced by so many and especially so at the Bosque Redondo. She also learned more about the Lipan Apache during these sessions and how they came to be part of the Mescalero reservation.

Eve stated in an interview when describing the old Scout, "Though frail and unable to speak English, he was mentally alert. Through his son, Percy, acting as interpreter, he agreed to give some accounts of his early life and also the legends of his people. Bigmouth, like many of his era, required his children to memorize the details of encounters in which parents or grandparents had participated."[6]

Percy had listened well and understood his people's history. His mother was Lipan, although they were now part of the Mescalero Apache tribe in an official capacity. She passed away in 1936, yet Percy kept her memory close and added her stories to his Mescalero repertoire.

As Eve soon discovered, the Lipan Apaches were indeed a force for much of the mid-1600s through the 1750s in Texas and borderland history. They were independent and well off, so they were attacked by many sources—all lesser tribes, according to both Bigmouths and also others with whom she spoke who were of Lipan lineage. For decades, there was constant conflict, so the Lipan, in a desire for survival as old as man himself, traveled farther south and east into Mexico, and some ventured west into New Mexico seeking peace and not war. However, the Lipan, in order to survive, turned their hunting skills into fighting skills. In their heyday, they were seen as fierce warriors, but eventually the culture of war always carried a price tag.

Percy's family survived via inter-marriage, and at this writing in 2014, the Lipan language is basically gone, along with most Lipan speakers. There is a small group in Texas that claims Lipan heritage, and they are trying to gather as much of their fragmented history as possible. Some recent histories have been published. Only a few at Mescalero recall their Lipan ancestry as vividly as did Percy and his father. Percy was correct in that he kept his tribal history and lore "in his sleeves," and his only hope of someday having this information put out in written form to share came through his friendship with a handful of individuals he met at Mescalero.

It should be recalled that Eve and others took down the information either with Gregg shorthand or tape recordings. These edited interviews remain true to the way the Old Apaches spoke English and are edited only for repetition, much like the folk tales. The heartfelt emotion and descriptions are as they related them to those with whom they spoke or trusted.

Eve learned about the Lipan struggles for self-identity. Percy's Lipan side was known as *Tuintsundé* or *Túntsande* ("Big Water People"), or the *Tú sis Ndé* band. They camped with several bands of Mescalero out on the Plains, where they gathered for hunting and raiding parties. By the late 1800s, the Lipan had become a scattered and almost destitute people, whereas the Mescaleros had moved onto their reservation lands and tried to adapt to a more structured life.

The Lipan were being driven southward by angry and strong groups of Comanches. The Spaniards made a halfhearted attempt to protect them through the construction of missions, but that ended when Comanche raids destroyed them. In desperation, the Lipans fled to lands along the Gulf Coast, learning to adapt and incorporate the good and bad aspects of living along coastal areas. That is when they became known as the Big Water people.

In addition to the threat from the Comanches, the scourge of smallpox also decimated them. The ugly scars of the disease were seen on many faces.

The Lipans continued their flight toward the south and west into the protective rugged Guadalupe Mountains of Texas and New Mexico. Here they became integrated over time with the Mescalero who ranged through this area. These Lipan then became known as the "No Water People." Others scattered into Mexico, living simple, desperately poor lives that led them to finally settle during the early 1900s in Mescalero.

Old Scout Bigmouth was adopted by his uncle, Chief Peso, as a strong-willed teenager. The patient Peso trained him and took him on raids and hunting trips into Mexico, showing him the old trails and camps where his parents and grandparents had lived and ultimately perished in conflicts with the Mexican military. They rode south mounted on strong horses they had stolen from the ever-present Comanche.

It is said Scout Bigmouth was born around 1855. We also know he was a stalwart young boy during the Bosque Redondo roundup that occurred about eight years later. He rode on horseback and helped his family during that tragic death march.

We also understand much better the relationship among the Lipan, Mescalero and Comanches from Bigmouth's perspective. They had stronger ties than previously indicated. They were, in many situations, like young siblings within a large and boisterous family. They fought hard and then worked together or intermarried until another argument caused friction and anger. Sometimes that anger resulted in war.

Bigmouth married a Lipan/Mescalero woman by the name of Eliza when he was about twenty, and they reared four sons. At age twenty-five, he became a scout at Fort Stanton and is on the rolls at the fort for at least two terms of service. Bigmouth, Shanta Boy and Crookneck all served as scouts during the Geronimo conflict.

Bigmouth had lived from the Stone Age well into that of the Atomic Age. He did not welcome such change. He had seen more in his one hundred years of living than was experienced by the human race previous to his birth. Like Percy, he was honored and respected by his people, yet he longed for the old ways, for the freedom and for the life that he knew before the Indian Wars and the great wars transformed the world.

In almost every interview, he spoke of similar events and happenings in the tried and true style given by Apaches down through the ages. He rarely varied his accounts. In one visit and interview he did, however, describe in a different way the Apache encounters with the "God Damns."

How the "God Damns" Took Away the Land and Dirtied the Water

Noted cowboy author Al F. Sinclair, late of El Paso, became another guest in the Bigmouth home. His interview was an eye opener for Sinclair. In May 1963, Sinclair wrote of his visit with the Bigmouth family. He entitled his article for the *Southwesterner* "Bigmouth's Father Remembered Happy Days, Before 'God-Damns' came to Dirty Water." The interview occurred on a summer day in 1957, a little over a year before "Old Dad" passed away. The Franciscan priest at the St. Joseph Mission Church informed Sinclair where the family lived.

'BIG MOUTH
MESCALERO APACHE
FORT STANTON
SCOUT
D. KUSIANOVICH

Drawing of old
Scout Bigmouth
by Dan
Kusianovich.
*Courtesy of Danna
Henderson and Eve
Ball.*

Sinclair had several hours of tape-recorded interview but for this article included only the more dramatic information that has paralleled what Eve Ball was told in a series of interviews with Percy translating. Mr. Sinclair located the same gray-colored cabin that Eve and I visited more than twenty years later when only Mack Bigmouth lived there.

On that day in 1957, it was Percy who answered the door. Percy was accustomed to people seeking out his elderly father, and so he asked Sinclair if he wished to speak with him. Taking him inside to the kitchen, Sinclair noted that there "sat the oldest man I had ever seen in my life!" Of course, he was over one hundred years of age at that time.

"Old Dad" was accustomed to questions about his past because Eve Ball and others had asked him to describe his early life. It was a good diversion because now the old warrior was blind and ancient, yet his memory was crisp and his sense of humor amazing. He always discussed the dreaded time of death at Fort Sumner. That was such a vivid memory that it was a given for any and all interviews. He also described the importance of water and how the Apache resented the way the white men from Fort Stanton dirtied their water supply. This was unforgivable, for the sweet water was a gift from *Ussen*, and the Sacred Mountain was a major watershed for so many. And he described their territory, a vast land that they considered their own before all the "God Damns" arrived.

Their chief, Natzili, had counseled them to try and like the "God Damns" (supposedly the cavalry men were called this because it was a term the Apaches heard the soldiers use all the time). When they held a council with the head military man, the Apaches explained how the water from the Rio Bonito was making them sick. They explained how they had, since long ago, used the water to drink, bathe and water their small fields. It always belonged to the Apache. The soldiers had moved way up there to the higher reaches of the mountain, and the water was being polluted.

They were told, "You don't like it, you move."

Then all the great chiefs of the Apaches got together on El Capitan to have a big talk. He said, "They talk one way, they talk another...then the greatest of them, Natzili, says we go to the Rio Feliz [near Roswell]. But that was long ago. We still preferred the Rio Bonito. That was our real home, the one to which we always returned. We roamed far in search of food, but we always returned to the beautiful little river that flowed from the White Mountain, one of our Sacred Mountains."[7] That interview was surely an eye opener for Mr. Sinclair.

Throughout every one of Bigmouth's interviews, there was always mention about the love for the rivers, and he spoke continually about the purity and sweet taste of this mountain water flowing from their sacred mountain.

Scout Bigmouth recalled on several occasions for Eve Ball with Percy translating:

> Ussen *made the land and gave it to the Apaches. Our country went north to the high mountains; and south as far as land was. We were a great nation with many bands. This was including both Mescalero and Lipan territory as well as that of the other bands like the Jicarilla, Chiricahua and Warm Springs.*

> *There were a few Mexican families in the valleys along the Bonito and Hondo, but we had little trouble with them. We traded skins and venison for guns and ammunition. When White Eyes came, trouble began and we learned the hard way that they fought each other, just as some Indian tribes did. They hunted us through the forests, our own forests, like wild animals.*
>
> *I remember how my parents frightened us by telling us the soldiers would get us. We learned to make no noise for fear that we might betray our hiding places to the White Eyes. They were a cruel, vicious people who cracked children's heads on wagon wheels and who attacked helpless women. They were worse than anything else—they were worse even than bears!*

The old scout always described with disgust that terrible man, General Carleton, saying, "The Apache have only stone weapons; the soldiers have long-range rifles. What chance do we have? For a long time, we fight and run; starve and run; then we hide and starve. We had nothing left for food; nothing left with which to fight. Our chief, Cadette, held a council with his men. And they decided it better to give up than for the women and children to die or to be cold and hungry. But that was wrong. Big mistake."

The Hellhole of the Bosque Redondo

Bigmouth said, "Kit Carson told us if we went to the Pecos around Fort Sumner, the army would feed us. We were dying a few each day and so finally all the warriors decided it better to live. That Pecos country not good, but we not hide, we not starve. So they dig a hole and Cadette and Carson, and all the mens in the council spit in that hole and cover it up to show that the troubles are buried and we at peace. Carson then tells us to bring everything we have to Fort Stanton and from there we began the long sad walk to Fort Sumner."

Throughout these interview sessions, Eve noted that as Percy translated, he would try not to show emotion, yet during certain descriptive parts of his father's narration, he looked old and haggard, almost as old as his father. She now understood the value of oral history even more because she later heard Percy recite events almost exactly as his father had told her. Many of these were the same accounts Percy passed on to his white friends in written or oral form. For example, in one session, the old scout said:

In the sad time [1863], I was a big boy. I think maybe about seven or eight. I was big enough to ride a horse and look after my mother. We had three horses and used one to pack our teepee and what few things we had. Most of our people had no horses, so they have to walk. And we Mescaleros are horse Indians. We don't like to walk.

We start on that sad journey, north. We go through Capitan Gap and north some more to the Pecos. Soldiers treat us very bad. They abuse the women and nobody to stop them! We cannot look at each other; we ashamed. Mescalero women are good; and they modest. We do not have any bad women and they victims of soldiers. No one stops them.

Eve vividly recalled the old man leaning forward and saying firmly to her, "You don't find that in the books or reports!"

Eve stated to me on many occasions that she felt ashamed to hear such terrible accounts of our treatment of the Apache, and especially of the women. Scout Bigmouth continued his story:

> *That place on the Pecos was a bad place. It was what you call a concentration camp today. It was not like our home. No mountains, no deer, no pines. Only a few cottonwoods. Antelopes out on the plains, but we are prisoners and cannot go hunt on the plains.*
>
> *The soldiers make us dig ditches. They make us dig the ground to plant corn. We not a farmer; we are a hunting and warrior peoples. And above all else, we were a free people. We never been penned up before. We unhappy, very unhappy. And hungry. Nothing but misery and hunger at that place. What man can bear to hear his child crying for food and do nothing?*
>
> *The worst thing is the water. On the White Mountain the water comes from the pure melting snow, and it is clear and cold; it is sweet and good. The Bonito water sweet and good.*
>
> *The Pecos water is muddy and it taste bad! It make us sick just to taste it. It make the horses sick. But there is no other water, so we have to drink. I remember water had a bad effect on us at first. I never got used to it. I went without water as long as I could stand the thirst. And when I did finally drink I gulped the water down as fast as I could to avoid the taste. I also remember going to bed hungry and waking up hungry.*[8]
>
> *One time they let our mens go hunt near the Guadalupes because they not want to feed us. Our warriors made a solemn promise to return to our families with food, and they kept that promise. They brought back many,*

Corrals at Fort Sumner depicting the poverty and extreme conditions encountered by the Apache POWs.
Courtesy Matt Barbour.

The pure, sweet mountain stream, the Bonito, in winter. Apaches revered this river, as did the Mogollon people before them.

many loads of meat and hides. We made teepee coverings and clothing, and we ate good venison and buffalo.

Sometimes the soldiers give us a little food, but never enough. A little tough beef, a little flour. We don't like wheat flour. And our buckskins wear out, and no deer to make more clothes. Every night a few of the young men run away, and some of the women; but the most of us stay, and we suffer.

We stay till they bring in the Navajos and put them above us on the Pecos. Maybe nine thousand and there were only about four hundred of us. We and Navajo are enemies. They steal our horses; and they fight us. But that is not the worst. One time they get the sickness from the soldiers—what you call smallpox. And they died, hundreds of them die. The soldiers throw the bodies in the river and they float down where we have to drink. We see them drift down. And worms in the water. Lots and lots of worms.

That was it. We leave. In the night we leave and take everyone. We go back to our own home on the Rio Bonito where no worms in the water.

Although written by a white man, the following poem, written just before World War I broke out, sums up the feelings so many had with regard to water. It is a common theme we see among our native peoples and very descriptive of the lands along the Bonito. It also depicts the reverence for the land felt by all caring people.

The Little Bonito, Child of the Snow

by P.G. Zimmerman

The Little Bonito is one of those pretty little mountain streams that rise amid the banks of snow in the White Mountains. Hence we call it "Child of the Snow."

Fort Stanton is a government Marine hospital and Sanitarium, and nestles on the banks of the Little Bonito 22 miles from the White Mountain. It was a military post from 1857–1897. The post now has a large herd of cattle, some horses, and mules, dairy farm and orchards and things too numerous to mention. The entire valley is irrigated from the Little Bonito which is verily the life of the valley…"

Flow on thou Little Bonito,
Scatter gladness wherever you go;
Fresh from thy home in the mountains;
And the beautiful drifts of snow.

Bear your silvery floods to the flowers
That so wildly bloom on the plain,
Be you their sweet soul and comfort,
Be you their sunshine and rain.

Come trickling down through Fort
    Stanton
'Mong the sleepy villas and trees;
Bless the tired hearts of the patients
That recline in their chairs of ease.

For they shall list in the evening
To your music so soft and low,
And in their hearts they will bless you
Chiquito Bonito, sweet waif of
    the snow.

Your course is so mild Bonito,
In your flight to the southern sea,
That pilgrims touched with your beauty
Have come to Live and die by thee.

They've come from the storm swept ocean;
The dark and heaving starless mane.
They've come to rest from the struggle,
Secure from life's worry, and pain.

Sing to them sweet Bonito;
Sing of the days so long gone past,
'Fore your waves were jarred by the drum,
Or stirring bugles war-like blast,

Sing again of a day to be,
When wars shall drench no more the sod,
When earth shall be one brotherhood;
The peaceful home of man and God.[9]

Bigmouth talked a lot about worms. We know about the maggots infesting dead bodies, but the cutworms that invaded the crops could have also contributed to his child's memory. Unfortunately, what had promised to be a good crop became infested with these devouring insects.

Rations for the Indians had to be cut to twelve ounces of flour and eight ounces of meat per day to ward off the threat of famine after both the 1864 and 1865 corn and wheat harvests were devastated.

Despite knowing that Carleton told the soldiers to kill escaping Apache men on sight, the Apaches packed up and began to leave under cover of night. Bigmouth stated:

> They want to kill all warriors. Even if they want to throw down their weapons and quit fighting…Soldiers don't want us round Fort Stanton

either for they need the land for their horses and cattle. They not want us to live there—not want us to live anywhere. Want all Apache dead. Soldiers take babies by heels and smash head on wagon wheel. "Nits make lice"—that's what Carleton and soldiers say. I know because some of our mens can understand White Eye talk. We pack up everything, we don't got much, and we carry it on our backs. Our horses died long ago. Perhaps we should have too? We take everybody, old peoples, babies, everybody. We leave in the night, very quiet. We leave fires burning and go. Soldiers follow us; they shoot and kill some womens. Old Lady Peso, she was a little girl then and she will tell you the same. Soldiers finally tell us to go to Fort Stanton. They count us and put tags on us. We don't get any food if we don't have tags. But they still don't give us food, and they tell us to come back in seven days. Seven days is a long, long time without food!

Bigmouth related another story about Apache suffering and sacrifice during the time they hid in the mountains and experienced the freezing cold with very few supplies and little hope after they escaped from the Bosque Redondo. Even though they had returned from the Bosque, times on the Bonito were not easy:

After the Bosque Redondo, we returned to the Bonito and camped upstream from the fort…When we camped, we scattered so that when the cavalry followed some might escape. We could not risk fires, so we ate what cold food we had and huddled for warmth. One old woman who had a blanket took several orphaned children and covered them with it. She had only a very little food, but gave each a mouthful; there was none left for her. She got them to sleep and hovered over them as best she could. When the men came at dawn, the children were safe, but she was dead.

There is a Native American proverb or *dicho* that describes that time: "The soul would have no rainbow if the eye had no tears."

Eventually, things got better, and the people became strong once again, for the Apache are a resilient people. However, it took many decades.

It is understandable that Bigmouth never wanted his parents or other family members to go hungry again. He was convinced to become a scout for the military while on a buffalo hunt across the Pecos. He was informed that if he should enlist, his family would be safe from further attacks by the soldiers. He would be permitted—even given—a rifle and ammunition, and he would receive eight dollars a month. He could actually purchase

Starving and ragged captives, taken c. 1886, Fort Bowie, Arizona. Note the extreme poverty and condition of these remnant Apaches.

The Old Scout was buried at the Mescalero Cemetery with the traditional white granite headstone given to all who served in the military. *Photo by Mary Serna.*

supplies. With this job, he would become self-sufficient, and that helped in his final decision.[10]

The young Bigmouth gave the idea prolonged thought before he finally enlisted. He despised the soldiers, but he also loved his family, and at that time, the scouts were not hated and resented like they were later during the final days before Geronimo's surrender. Bigmouth served honorably and in later years always wore his scout military medal when he could. He married and reared four sons, of whom Percy was the eldest.

Chapter 3

PERCY BIGMOUTH'S GIFTS (1891–1959)

Probably I'll be one of the first Indians to subscribe for the Ruidoso News.
—*Percy Bigmouth, letter to the editor of the* Ruidoso News *on May 31, 1946*

It is certainly not an exaggeration to claim that Percy was one of the best-known and most beloved individuals on the reservation.
—*Eve Ball*

Percy had several gifts bestowed upon him in his life. One was being a good storyteller, and another was the gift of responsibility. He felt he should care for his elderly father and keep the legends and lore of his fellow Apaches "in his sleeves" so they would not become lost over time. His interest, his disposition and his memory served him well in this quest.

Percy would also agree with a favorite Native American proverb: "A people without a history is like wind over buffalo grass."

Many today consider it to be a tragedy that these wonderful folk stories are simply gone from everyday life. For the most part, they have disappeared from the world of the people who created them, and we are the losers.

As we have learned, Percy often wrote the tales for his friends during the winter months at Mescalero. This cold-weather tradition of Apache storytelling was done in accordance with the cycles of nature. One worked, hunted and moved during spring, summer and fall. During winter, one gathered about the campfires and told stories and learned from the elders. Of course, there were few campfires during those years, so he wrote them

Left: Percy in traditional buckskin clothing. *Courtesy Harris family.*

Below: Percy standing by car. Unlike many Apaches of that era, Percy knew how to drive. *St. Joseph Apache Mission.*

sitting next to his wood stove, mailed them out and in so doing helped preserve his own favorites or the ones he felt were pertinent to his tribe.

While it is difficult to separate the two men, father and son, in terms of family legacy and events that affected them, Percy was clearly an individual who understood the twentieth century. He spoke English, drove, subscribed to newspapers and believed in the significance of good public education for every child in addition to the traditional education provided by tribal elders. In a letter to Gene written on October 4, 1940, he stated, "Schooling is hard work, but it is good for everybody. I never have been [to] school myself, my grade is just third. That all, here at old Mescalero...I made a badly mistake, for not gone back to school. I need a good whipping for that."

Percy cared for his aged father and sacrificed a great deal for this act of kindness and parental responsibility. "Old Dad" was from the era of the Bosque Redondo tragedy and the sorrow of an Indian people slowly

Percy, far right in buckskins, with Eve, far left, and old Crookneck and Scout Bigmouth on front porch of the Bigmouth home.

being squeezed onto lands that were a mere shadow of what the expanses of Apachería covered. Percy appreciated and revered this history, and that legacy is what he attempted to preserve while struggling to survive in the White Man's world. That was not an easy task.

Little did Percy understand that he would become a primary heir to the struggles and the survival of his family and ultimately the keeper of not only the family history but tribal heritage as well. The military history, in particular, has been written about ad nauseum. However, Percy extended that heritage by relating many of the folk tales and legends that carried a more positive message depicting a different side to Apache history.

In 1924, another significant event occurred for the Native Americans. They were granted citizenship, but mostly they did not reap those benefits until much later because they hardly understood what had happened to them culturally or linguistically after the Apache Wars ended in 1886. The concept of "citizenship" was totally foreign to them.[11]

Although Percy did not realize it at the time, he was swimming against the tide of cultural disintegration.

Percy was reluctant to go into any detail when discussing his own background. However, Eve learned that as a small child, he loved to ride horses, as did most Apache children. He had even discussed with her the important role of the horse to his people. His father, "Old Dad," had always said, as did many of the pre-reservation warriors, "We Mescaleros are horse Indians. We don't like to walk."

Percy understood that the horse was brought to the New World by the Spanish conquistadors. He also told a tale regarding this magnificent animal. No native people had ever seen such a fearsome and strong creature, especially in those first years when they also saw men riding the strange beast. Later, they learned how to temper the horse and made rapid use of the animal's fleetness of foot and ability to carry heavy loads for long distances. The Apaches quickly converted from walkers to riders. The following is his account given to Eve Ball.

The Horse and Our People

They say that the horse was created for mens. Along with this special relationship sadly came war, greedy mens and hard times; Some good times too when we win.

My mother's people, the Lipan, and my Dad's, the Mescaleros, always had a good feeling for the horse, and once they learned how to tame him then stories about how the horse came to them became legend too; This story talk about how horse came to us and how he looked. This came about way before our tribes came to where we live now.

Lightening [sic] was placed in the horse's nose to create the hot breath; rain and the rainbow were used to make horse's hooves. This very important for our rough country; hard hoof allow escape; The eye was made from the first star [evening] and the early moon [crescent] became the horse's fine tipped ears; and they say to make horse all powerful, the Creator, Ussen, gave horse strength from whirlwind. Whirlwind came from each of our four sacred directions; and gave horse strong legs and heart; hips and shoulders.

With this energy the horse came to be and could run and run like whirlwinds; horse was great help to the Apache of olden times. In those days before our modern times; Old Dad knew this was so because they traveled back and forth to Mexico on horseback; they fought the soldiers and escaped many times. The horse was very valuable to us in those days, and sometimes now; but not so much as then.[12]

Percy saddling his horse. *Courtesy St. Joseph Apache Mission.*

Percy had another horse-related story from the Lincoln County War years when Billy the Kid and his gang were wreaking havoc everywhere. War once more meant violence, and mostly the white men blamed the Indians if their horses were stolen, although many times it was a group of rogues and outlaws who were the real thieves. Percy's story and one from relatives of early Hispanic residents converge to present a different side of Billy the Kid and the Apache trying to protect their horses from men such as Billy.

The following tale was recorded by the author during interviews with Eve Ball and Mauro Sánchez. It involved Apolonio Sedillo and his pal Billy.

Billy the Kid Steals from the Apaches

Cuentos (folk stories) of the exploits of Billy the Kid were recounted by the Mexican people (early Hispanic residents of Lincoln County 1848–1881) with great delight, for he was truly loved by the quiet settlers who spoke a different tongue than the more aggressive and corrupt men who had recently moved into the territory. Nevertheless, he was a rogue, and he had no use for or understanding of the Apaches who also shared the landscape and country around Fort Stanton. Sharing the feeling of many Anglos of the day, Billy the Kid believed the Apaches were "*el enemigo,*" the enemy.

Before the Lincoln County War emerged as a serious conflict, Billy and some of his compadres delighted in stealing horses from everyone, including the Apaches who were living

Billy the Kid. *Illustration by Bob Boze Bell, executive editor,* True West.

near Fort Stanton in their peaceful camps. Percy Bigmouth had, in translating for his father, related one such story. These losses were becoming too great because horses were a valued part of their culture. The soldiers did nothing. Finally, to prevent any more loss, the Apaches built huge brush corrals to keep the thieves at bay. However, that still did not deter Billy and his men. It only made them more careful and determined.

One evening, a grand trick was played by Billy and a man named Apolonio Sedillo. Everyone thought it was a clever prank that luckily did not end in bloodshed.

Members of Billy's gang must have had one too many tequilas, so they decided they would have some entertainment by stealing horses and mules from the Apaches.

As Apolonio described it, they crept through a large break in the corral and into camp, where they noticed one old mule was tied by a rawhide rope inside a teepee. No doubt this must have been a very valuable animal to be tied up this way. Billy wanted to steal it come hell or high water. However, there was one problem: a barking dog made so much ruckus that they had to retreat before the Apaches discovered their presence. They waited for a while and then Billy came up with this idea of throwing the dog some extra *sopaipillas* (a traditional fried bread much like a donut without sugar). He kept them in his saddle bag. In this way, the men crept up to the mule, cut the rope and Billito rode him out of camp *pronto*! Other *caballos* were also taken, and from there, they drove the stolen stock and that mule to a favorite hideout called Ratón Springs, way over in the Capitan mountains. They stayed around Ratón for a few days with José Montoya's brother-in-law. From Ratón, they drove the ponies to Chisum's ranch near Roswell, New Mexico.

Thus, we have a rather amusing story corroborating Percy's frustrated and angry account of how Billy seemed to get away with stealing their horses. Naturally, the locals thought the *sopaipilla* story to be humorous.

We also know the Apaches were aware of Billy and his gang's activities from reports and interviews years later. Eric Tortilla once told Eve Ball that the Kid and his gang got so bad the Apaches unsuccessfully demanded to be protected. He also stated that several Mescaleros who worked with Mexican cowboys and loggers said that the Hispanics all claimed that Billy did not die. That was more than forty years after he was supposedly killed by Pat Garrett.[13]

Ironically, in light of his love and respect for horses, a horse may have caused Percy permanent physical damage when he was very young. When his mother rode, he would often accompany her across the vast lands of the Mescalero reservation. Though her mount was gentle, the horse spooked one bitterly cold afternoon when a calf jumped up beside their trail, and Percy was thrown into a rocky arroyo. An injury to the spine caused him to be hunchbacked, and when fully grown, he was only an inch or so over five feet. Several people who knew Percy have commented about his short stature.

Dr. Jackson Harris, husband of Gene Neyland, wrote in a letter dated April 14, 1981, "P.S. Parenthetically, Mrs. Ball mentioned Percy's spine. Although I was only a medical student at the time that I spent most of my time with Percy, it was my impression that he probably had Potts Disease, which is tuberculosis of the spine which causes destruction of some of the vertebrae."

Whatever the reason, Percy became shy and self-conscious about his physical appearance. He worked very hard and cared for his family, but he never married. After his mother's death, he assumed the responsibility of caring for his aged father and continued working at the ranger station.

Years earlier, Percy's father had required all of his sons to memorize the Apache legends and history, as was the proper oral tradition among the Apaches for centuries. He also learned from his father to become an expert in many Apache crafts, although in the pre-reservation times, these crafts were considered to be part of their survival, such as the making of baskets, bows and arrows, lances and shields. Percy made beautiful bows and arrows carried in quivers made of mountain lion or deer hide. He was an expert in basket making and in tanning and beading buckskin. He often made eagle-feather bonnets. His fame spread, and it brought many individuals to the reservation to interview him. Among them were numerous Boy Scout masters who flocked to the Bigmouth home, especially in the summer, when people from the arid plains and parched deserts sought refuge—as they do today—in the cool, pine-clad Ruidoso highlands. There was a hunger for these skills among the younger generation who came to see him at the old ranger station.

There were some among the Apache who preferred no contact with the White Man—and understandably so. However, Percy left the arrogance and ignorance of others behind as he sought to teach about his traditions and left a lasting impression of grace, dignity and humor. Thus, from the mid-

Percy Bigmouth at the ranger station. *Courtesy Harris family.*

1930s to the early 1950s, Percy worked with any who cared to learn, and in the winter months, he corresponded with friends like Mary and Gene. There were others too, but unfortunately, they are long forgotten and we do not have their names. There may have been other accounts that have not survived or remain hidden in boxes or trunks.

During the summer, according to Eve Ball, Percy was able to provide adequately for the family's needs. This included chopping wood for their cook stove. But in the winter months, his frail body was often unequal to the task. There were days when both he and his elderly father spent most of their daylight hours in bed or by the wood stove because they were unable to heat their entire home properly. Eve had learned about this years after Percy's death, for he was too proud to tell her this difficulty. It is likely that he did not tell his family either, because they would have come to his aid if they had known.

This task of recording the old stories kept him going, so to speak. One can barely imagine what it was like in the cabin where the family lived, with "Old Dad" usually in bed and Percy at the kitchen table writing these legends for his friends from memory in pencil on the Big Chief tablets so commonly used in those days.

Eve Ball always stated that the Apaches had better memories than the white people had. They were trained, much as "Old Dad" had trained Percy, to pay attention and to memorize because during war or out on a hunt, their lives depended on the accurate descriptions or relaying of messages. And although we consider their stories and legends much as we would our own "fairy tales," to an individual like Percy, they represented the history of his Apache people through many centuries.

Percy was also considered by some to be a "holy man." One individual remembered him fondly and with great respect and affection, calling him "grandfather," as many do when referring to an older individual, although they may not be related in that manner.

Percy's handwriting is also the subject of commentary, for although he received limited education at one of the Bureau of Indian Affairs–funded "Indian schools," his calligraphy was truly beautiful. Eve always referred to his long flowing lines as "Spencerian" or classic. He encouraged all with whom he corresponded to continue their education, and one can see a hint of his own desire to have had more access to a formal education.

Percy wrote to Mary Montgomery on January 19, 1950, "How you like your new school, Is the lesson all easy for you? Imagine its hard but I'm saying, Study hard, and you get to the top, In some of these fine days!" He mentions Christmas and Santa Claus, asks about her brother and ends stating that his brothers, Mack and Harry, were getting along okay.

In another letter to Ms. Montgomery written on February 15, 1950, he once again reiterated how he missed his friends and said that he was taking time to write letters now because of the cold.

With your hard lessons. That it, Mary. Study hard, some of these fine days, you reach to the top! Do your level best, as the great chance is all yours; While you are young and willing to take up the hard struggle; Throw it on your strong shoulder; Don't let the hard lesson down and fall under, Stand up and free it…After you finish your schooling, I believe teaching is okay; Though sometime there are one or two hard boil eggs in the class; but still I've think teacher is alright.

Percy then switched gears and talked about Mary living out on a ranch. We can verify that Percy believed country living is much better for all concerned:

> *So now you live out on the ranch, where the coyote are howling. That good; yes living out in the country is much better I think, where you can go out on a horseback ride, Living in the town, I've kinda think spending lots money; that way I look at. A person have to dress up neat too; But out in the country, a person can live wild and woolie; How you like your new home in Piñon. Good grazing country I suppose! Bear out there when I were a tiny kid, Way back in 1892, when the Indians used to go out hunting, out that country clear to the Guadalupe Mountains, now we can't do that anymore. At one time all that country belong to us Mescalero Apache; They used to go clear down to Roswell and to Pecos river to hunt antelope, I hear down there too. We came down to Roswell once when very few houses were there, I still remember that. We trade some buckskin and moccasins for some gun shell and food. That was my very younger days. Today Roswell is big city; Now about the moccasin you were talking about, I tell you Mary, I'll do my very level best to look for a pair, see what I can find.*

He also wrote to Gene Neyland about doing well in school. In a letter written on April 24, 1947, he said, "Well Gene do your level best, while you are young and study your hard good lesson, throw it on your strong shoulder, and reach for the top, push your class aside and be on ahead of them."

Note the similar wording and expressions of repetition as he wrote to both Mary and Gene.

He also sent a letter to the editor of the *Ruidoso News* on May 31,

Mary Spencer Montgomery. *Courtesy Mary Montgomery.*

1946, stating that he found it to be a good paper and that he will be one of their subscribers: "Probably I'll be one of the first Indians to subscribe for the *Ruidoso News*." Once again, this is indicative of his desire to read and be informed as much as possible.

One other point that should be made is that Percy was a gentleman, and it is interesting to note that, at least in the pages of written material, Percy never sent to his friends any vulgar or provocative stories, though those kinds of tales were recorded by anthropologists of the time. For example, vulgar stories have been listed under Stories of Foolish People, Unfaithfulness and Perversion. Indeed, after reading some of these recorded by Opler and others, one can understand why Percy did not write down any such tales for Mary, Gene or Eve.

The hundreds of tourists who came to visit Percy with preconceived ideas departed with their hearts full of unique stories and their souls refreshed with the wonderful and beautiful lands surrounding Sierra Blanca. These visitors were a gift for Percy, and his teachings were gifts to them in return.

That all changed in 1950 when Percy realized that "Old Dad" could no longer care for himself. He was over ninety-four, and though it was a difficult decision because he so enjoyed the company and the tourists who came to visit, Percy decided to quit his job as a ranger for the tribe. In so doing, his personal sacrifice was great, but he knew he had to look after the elderly patriarch. With that act, he often sank into depression and sadness. We now understand that the letters and the folklore he tried to record and the people coming for interviews helped him cope with a difficult situation.

At the age of 108 (records vary on this) in late November 1958, "Old Dad" died. Tragically, a few weeks later, Percy was stricken with a heart attack and passed away in an ambulance en route to Fort Stanton Hospital. He kept asking the ambulance driver when they would arrive. Percy died as the ambulance drove into the fort grounds. His family connections with Fort Stanton from the old times to the present were still very much a part of his life and death. He was sixty-eight.

Chapter 4

THE COVETED HAVEN

*The Ruidoso Highlands always provided a coveted haven for people from the
hot desert country beginning with the early hunters and gatherers, the Jornada
Mogollon, Apaches and pioneer settlers who came much later.*
—*Eve Ball, 1980 presentation before officers' wives at Holloman Air Force Base*

In the 1930s, Ruidoso was a tiny rural mountain village located at the edge
of the Mescalero Apache reservation. It was a community surrounded by
natural beauty, and like the community of its neighbors, the Mescaleros, it
was always within view of the 12,003-foot Sierra Blanca. Residents became
one with this environment, and while visitors came for a while and then
departed, always the Apaches—as well as the steadfast Hispanic and Anglo
pioneer families—remained. That was the way of things.

As we have seen, three unique individuals (Eve Ball, Mary Montgomery
and Gene Harris) became conduits for Percy Bigmouth to pass on tribal
traditions. Just who were these individuals who also came to the coveted
mountain haven?

Eve: The Saddle Maker

Though Eve Ball came into Percy's life after he met Mary and Gene,
she became for him and "Old Dad"—as well as numerous others—what

Eve Ball telling a story, circa 1980.

she likened to a saddle maker. Eve noted that before the saddle was designed and made, she needed the tree of the saddle, the stirrups, the leather rigging and cinch straps. The Apaches and their accounts were to be considered the parts. Once she obtained them, Eve then set about constructing the saddle (or the book). It was only through their bringing to her the very important sections of that saddle that she could create a beautiful and strong work of art.

By the time she met Percy and his father, Eve had been in the process of interviewing, studying, gathering information and learning about the Apaches. For more than three decades, Eve Ball listened to the Apache people. She gained their respect and ultimately their friendship. And by listening rather than trying to talk over the old-timers, she obtained fresh information and a differing point of view. That new perspective is what makes her books timeless.

Many elders indicated that Eve Ball was a "gutsy" lady with a lot of grit. The descendants of early Hispanic settlers built her an adobe home in Ruidoso and became her friends for life. The Apaches called her the "old white lady with many stories," and they came to her with some of their own history. Percy was one of those elders. All three cultures shared with her their "stories of survival" during difficult times, especially when the winds of war swept over the region.

Eve Ball's long life spanned two centuries, the nineteenth and the twentieth, and upon her death in 1984, at the age of ninety-four, a vast reservoir of knowledge and history of our beloved Southwest and, in particular, southeastern New Mexico was lost. Much like that of Percy, though, her writing was saved for future generations. She also fortunately incorporated many of Percy and Scout Bigmouth's accounts into her notes, files, articles and books.

When questioned about her own life, Eve was as elusive as the rugged ranchers and valiant Apaches she wrote about in numerous best-selling classics. Her roots encompassed the South and the plains of Kansas and Texas, and ultimately, the lure of New Mexico brought her to the Ruidoso Highlands after World War II, much as the highlands had enchanted the families of Mary and Gene.

Eve Ball as a
young woman,
circa 1915.

Eve Ball, seated in center with long western dress, entertaining friends, circa 1970.

Eve had traveled throughout New Mexico many times and always had the desire to find a niche that would fulfill the ambition she had since childhood to write about the Apache. The mountain village of Ruidoso proved to be that niche. Not only were the beautiful natural surroundings appealing, but the Mescalero Apache Reservation was nearby. Eve was also an avid gardener, so she searched for a special site that would allow her to be creative and at one with her surroundings. She eventually purchased property near Nob Hill. Wild Castilian roses cascaded blossoms of creamy gold during the spring, and purple-hued irises, apricot trees, peonies of all colors and fragrant lilacs added their subtle beauty. Beyond that, she allowed the natural environment to remain intact. It was a sanctuary for wildlife, and of course, for Eve, it became her new home.

She still had to make a living, so she ran an antique store out of her home and had a few apartments constructed around the property. Leasing them out to seasonal visitors to the pine-clad mountain country, she made ends meet. At the same time, she settled into writing, research and, of course, interviewing. Included were incredible tales of people's strength and survival in a rough and rebellious country. Oftentimes, she was overwhelmed by the power of their accounts and knew she must incorporate them into viable narratives of their world, their time and their place.

Long before the concept of studying one's roots became popular, Eve insisted in her quiet manner on learning the history of the Anglos, Apaches and Hispanics. She became respected and trusted by all three groups and impressed upon all the importance of preserving this information as part of their heritage. Her sincere interest led many reticent pioneers to bring her their papers, family photos and treasured mementos, thus fleshing out their versions of events.

To obtain the Apache story took about two decades. It took that long to research and to know the participants of the Apache Wars before she was ready to write about the Mescalero, Lipan and Chiricahua. The Apaches also well remembered the lost freedom, broken promises and bitter years of exile from their beloved southwestern homelands. By patience and an honest desire to learn from the Apaches, Eve won the confidence of over sixty-seven tribal elders. They trusted her and believed she would tell *their* history from *their* side, not only the side presented by their enemies. While she documented and included the military point of view, it often differed from that of the Apaches. If one were to describe the Apache version using their words and worldview, one often went against the military accounts, especially of conflicts during the war years and those of imprisonment.

Eve had learned about the Bosque Redondo from Scout Bigmouth. Another stunning story of survival and renewed freedom came from Ace Daklugie, who had been a prisoner of war for twenty-seven years (1886–1913). In a poignant 1955 interview, the nephew to Geronimo and son of Chief Juh of the Nednhi narrated the following account. It was the first time he had shared this personal story with a White Eye.

Apparently, just before Daklugie surrendered along with other Apaches in 1885, he had taken his war club and walked up a nearby ridge. Knowing he may never see his beloved homeland again, he had decided on his final act of defiance. His enemies would not strip him of all of his weapons. The war club was a good-sized rock large enough to fit in one's hand, with leather sewn about it and placed on a strong handle of wood. Hiding it behind a large boulder, and memorizing the location, the young warrior of seventeen then calmly walked down the ridge and into legend. Sadly that day, they all prepared to surrender to the hated White Eyes.

After twenty-seven years as a POW, he returned to his beloved Southwest. One of the first things Daklugie did was to return to the ridge, locate the boulder, dig into the earth and retrieve his war club. The wooden handle

Ramona Chihuahua Daklugie, the daughter of Chief Chihuahua and wife of Ace Daklugie, in her buckskin wedding dress, is an absolutely beautiful example of the pride and the stunning beauty of the Apache women. Good friends for many years, Ramona helped open doors for Eve Ball to interview Apaches at Mescalero.

had rotted, and the leather was partially gone. He reworked the leather and replaced the handle. For more than forty years, he had kept it at his home with other treasured mementos, until one afternoon during an interview with Eve in 1955, he handed it to her as a gift. Telling the story to Eve, he stated that he felt truly liberated and no longer a POW once he had obtained this symbol of his days of freedom as a youth and a free Apache.

Daklugie and others from that era could well relate to the powerful Bosque Redondo tragedy recounted by Old Scout Bigmouth and Percy. They saw it happen before their very eyes. It is amazing that they were not more embittered or filled with disgust at what they observed and experienced.

Eve frequently stated that she made no judgment calls—it was a different era, and one had to view things from that historical frame of reference, not our own. At least, that was her philosophy, and ultimately, it was a successful one. The old ones confided in her as they had no other person. She did not break that trust.

"If nothing else is said about me," Eve once stated, "I want people to understand and know about my long struggle to get my books published. Oral history was laughed at then. Most PhDs never fully acknowledged the

In 1982, Eve Ball, at age ninety-two, received from U.S. senator Pete Domenici a Joint Congressional Resolution honoring her body of work (research, history and books).

intrinsic value of oral accounts until the past few years. But it was almost too late, for those who actually experienced that history are gone." However, not before Eve Ball recorded many of their accounts, and not before Percy passed on his legends and folktales to his white friends.

When Eve passed on to the land beyond the shining mountains on Christmas Eve 1984, she received one last tribute. In a special service at St. Joseph Apache Mission, the magnificent stone church and veterans' memorial in the heartland of Mescalero Apache country, old friends presented music and eulogies in both English and Apache. This magnificent stone cathedral was built by her friend of many years, Father Albert Braun (the hero priest of Corregidor). It was also the church where Percy had been confirmed in 1918 and where his family felt at home for decades.

Donalyn Torrez and Silas Cochise read special Apache prayers or translated English words into their beloved language. Father Larry, newly arrived Franciscan priest at Mescalero, presented a wonderful eulogy and service too, for he had gone among Eve's many friends and inquired about this woman and learned how the Apaches remembered her. Others spoke eloquently about her legacy. Though it was a cold and dreary December, it might also be noted that both "Old Dad" and Percy had passed away during the cold months, but the warmth of their memory no doubt kept many from feeling the icy fingers of winter on those sad days as well. The words of friends, family and colleagues reminded everyone of their legacy.

Dr. David Townsend, long a favorite among students of New Mexico history, declared that the beauty and symmetry of history must be presented so that our younger generation must not turn away from their gloriously instructive past. In that, Percy, Eve, Mary and Gene would agree.

Although Eve Ball's adobe home, once surrounded by wild Castilian roses and many native flowers, will no longer be a meeting place where people gather to recite their legends or speak about history and "the way of things," a lone, stately spruce stands as a symbol of this talented and dedicated woman. Like that magnificent tree, Eve Ball often stood alone throughout her ninety-four years. The tree was planted more than thirty years before her death by Daklugie. He had brought it to her as a surprise for one of the few white people he had ever respected.

———

Similarly, Mary and Gene, in their special manner and desire to become educated about the Apache way, also made no judgment calls. They took Percy for what he was and proved to him that they were interested in learning, not simply taking. Though they were from a different generation than Eve and Percy, we find there are always a few within each generation who create a bridge to the past. It is fortunate for us that they also became part of the story.

Though from different generations, the two younger girls, Mary and Gene, spent the summers from 1938 to the early 1950s in a similar routine. Gene's account began in 1938 and Mary's a bit later. They spent a good portion of their time riding and enjoying the benefits of the beautiful and colorful mountain environment. At that time, people, young and old, were much more into riding, hiking and living in the "Wild West." Dude ranches, wranglers and cowboy music dominated the scene. Hats, boots, saddles and campfires were part of that era as well. It was a less complicated time, and both girls enjoyed their "coveted haven." Their families also maintained cabins in Ruidoso for decades.

In their correspondence, one can observe that the feeling for what they learned and experienced is much the same.

Mary: Special Friend

Mary Spencer Montgomery was also drawn into the circle because her family had a cabin in this lovely land. She now lives in Texas but continues to visit the Ruidoso Highlands. Mary Serna and I spent a delightful day with Ms. Montgomery in July 2013, discussing those days and touring the family cabin that is still in their possession after one hundred years. It was a privilege to meet this lovely lady in person.

She mentioned her love for New Mexico and said that her father, Colonel Flournoy Poindexter Spencer, a transplant from Mississippi, married her Roswell, New Mexico mother. At one time, her father was a tuberculosis patient at Fort Stanton, having contracted the dreaded "white plague" during World War I.

She wrote later:

Mary Montgomery at the family cabin near the Mescalero Reservation. *Photo by Mary Serna.*

You are stirring up long forgotten memories and I am enjoying it. Cannot remember how old I was to know—or realize—why each time I would be at the Indian cabin with Percy—all the Apache women and children would run and close themselves in the cabin. In those days no Indian women would have anything to do with us. Such a shame. I would so have liked to have some of them to play with as many summers not many my age were around our cabin. In those years I was about 7 or 8—got my first horse at 6 and it was 1 mile from our cabin to the Ranger cabin. If only they had known how much I wanted to be a friend as I was to Percy.

Percy would tell me the old stories—the one I remember most is about their encampment in Florida and the journey back and the days in various areas of the region before their placement on the present reservation.

I am so glad you are doing this research! Percy was a warm, gentle person and very kind to "little white girls" that bothered him constantly. Long, long ago. Thanks for listening.

In another e-mail, she writes:

At the Indian cabin, on the screened in porch, we would try to teach others our card games. I mentioned before his coming to lunch once a summer. We enjoyed that too. The folks used to talk about how, on horseback, he could so quietly sneak up on a fisherman and then ask to see his license. He tried to teach me, but both my horse and I could never master this trait. I was always amazed at Percy's ability in that way.

Here is another flash back which is rather funny. One day as a few of us were heading up to the reservation for a day's ride—this time on the middle fork of the river—not far from the Indian Ranger cabin we found Percy and Mack (his brother) on their backs half way under a large rock by the trail and they were hand painting "whatever" under the rock? We all stopped and talked and laughed at them a few minutes and then went on with the ride. Something for the tourist—who knows—but it was a little strange. Should have asked Percy later about it. Never did.

No doubt there were other stories about his work with Boy Scouts and tourists, teaching them how to sneak up on a person and then realizing how clumsy White Eyes are and taking it in good stride when they failed that test. He was welcomed to many campfire programs, where he was often the guest, and he loved to talk of the old ways. Even though Percy was very small in stature, probably owing to his spinal injury, he was surely tall in their eyes.

Gene: Keeper of the Records

According to Dr. Harris, Gene's husband, in correspondence on October 12, 1987, "Gene's mother and aunt were both school teachers [*sic*], one from Texas, the other from Wisconsin. They purchased a cabin in Ruidoso in the late 1930's [*sic*] where they spent the summers as so many Texas people did to escape the summer heat. Gene...made many, many full day trips to Baldy and back. The Mescalero Ranger Station...was just inside the reservation."

Gene noted that she loved horses so much that her mother would rent one for her "by the season."

At that time, Wendell's Stables were where people rented horses. The ride took them through the reservation, past the Bigmouth home, up to where all riders had to sign in at the ranger station. Though called a ranger station, it was not on Forest Service lands but Mescalero lands. The "ranger" was Percy Bigmouth.

In a telephone interview, Gene recalled:

Gene and her husband, Dr. Jackson Harris.
Courtesy Harris family.

In the late thirties, there were few tourists so we were quite the curiosity. The first time I saw Percy was at the ranger station. I began to recognize some of the other Apaches and their children, but it was Percy who befriended me. The signing-in process took over half an hour, and I began to talk to him while I waited for the others. He must have sensed my interest for he told me many things about his people. I learned to especially love the Coyote stories, as well as other adventures of various animal and super human characters.

If I had been more knowledgeable about Apache history I would have known what to ask. I feel certain that Percy would have told me much more. However, I am fortunate to have had his friendship over the years until his death. The versions he sent to me of the Coyote and Creation legends and of the Lipan-Comanche battles will always be a treasure, and I hope they can one day be shared with others of my race as well as his own. Both my husband and I hope that by sharing this memento of the past, a bridge to better understanding of the two cultures will ensue.

It was Gene who fully captured the heart of the tribal elder. Although he had corresponded with several White Eyes over the years, it was to Gene that he mailed his pages and pages of stories. And it was not difficult to be drawn to this lovely young woman who blossomed and, long after her final departure from New Mexico to her new home in Tennessee, became a charming addition to the Harris family.

Martha Gene Neyland was born on June 17, 1926, in Cuero, Texas, and she passed away on October 25, 2009. Her obituary noted that Gene graduated from Austin High School and the University of Texas. Earning a bachelor's degree in child development, she was also a member of the Delta Gamma sorority. According to her family, she loved to play bridge,

Above: Gene on her horse, Phoenix. *Courtesy Harris family.*

Right: Gene seated on a rock near their cabin, 1939. *Courtesy Harris family.*

Gene in Percy's War Bonnet, Mescalero Ranger Station, 1939. *Courtesy Harris family.*

garden and cook. She adored babies, children, animals and her family, and that was evident from her days in Ruidoso. Her warmth, loving good nature and sense of humor were mainstays. She and Dr. Jackson Harris were married for sixty-one years. Dr. Harris still comes to New Mexico to visit his Albuquerque family.

In phone conversations with her in the late 1980s, I also found her to be very helpful. She generously mailed me extra photos of her family and her husband, who enjoyed visits to their now shared coveted haven.

Gene's marriage left a void in Percy's life, especially once she and her husband stopped coming to the Ruidoso Highlands. Loneliness sometimes drives people to sadness, anger or depression. For Percy, however, it was a return to the oral traditions of his people. He also began to correspond, and while his letters were few and far between, his folklore accounts turned into many pages in three Big Chief tablets. Percy apparently did not feel too self-conscious when writing these stories for his friends. He acknowledged his poor grammar: "I'm here, write a few more Indian Legend and myth which my Lipan peoples used to tell their children. It's a night story. You see, we don't have no written story, like the White peoples have; so I'm trying my level best. I'm sure I make lot of mistaken. But I can't help it, I need someone to help me; but I thought I do it alone; as there no one around to help. But

Gene in pioneer parade, Ruidoso, 1940. *Courtesy Harris family.*

hope who ever look over my story; hope they enjoyed it, and the mistaken; here I may ask to correct my error; as my English is awful and poor."

Dr. Harris wrote to me: "I am a native of Albuquerque and frequently travel home and could hand carry the manuscript." He also stated that his only request was "that the manuscript be returned when you are through with it." By "manuscript," Dr. Harris meant the three tablets. Eventually, however, we decided to have Xerox copies mailed to me. I reviewed them long ago and now after thirty years once again.

In April 1949, Percy wrote to Gene:

> *This is my Indian story which I written down for my White friends. I only wish that someone would help, but no one, so I do the best I can. I'm half Lipan Apache and half Mescalero. Lipan Apaches used to live down here in Texas, Austin clear down to Gulf of Mexico. They all left their country, gone across Rio Grande River on to the Mexico side. At last they*

can't get along with the Mexicans So they left back across the Rio Grande River on the north side. Finally they started up the North and stop with the Mescalero Tribe, So today we are here.

We are glad to live with the Mescalero. Now the Mexico don't bother us. They used to make a raid, and capture the children and women killing the mens. My Dad is Mescalero, but my mother is Lipan. She died August 24, 1936. Only Dad is with us. He's the oldest among the Mescalero, he's around 93 right now, and I got three brothers they all younger than myself, I'm the oldest of the four brothers.

Now hope you enjoy this Lipans [Mescalero] my explanation story; and correct the story, Fill it up with the right word That it fit the story.

Written by
Percy Bigmouth
Mescalero, New Mexico
Thanks!

Dr. Harris wrote on May 14, 1981, "Again, I very much appreciate your interest and that of Mrs. Ball and I hope that Percy's stories can be preserved. As he says, 'Iron them out good.'"

Like Percy, I have kept this project "in my sleeves" and now plan to unroll them and to "iron them out good." Hopefully I have achieved that goal.[14]

As Rudyard Kipling stated, "If History were taught in the form of stories, it would never be forgotten." In that Percy, Eve, Mary and Gene would agree.

Part II

"I Kept It in My Sleeves" (As Told by Percy Bigmouth and Eve Ball)

Chapter 5

THE LEGEND OF CREATION

Sacred pollen, hoddentin, was scattered along the face of the heavens, forming the Milky Way.
—*Apache medicine man, Mescalero*

Honor the sacred. Honor the Earth, our Mother. Honor the Elders. Honor all with whom we share the Earth.
—*author unknown*

Imagine, if you will, a roaring campfire on a cold December night. The children are up front nestled close by the storyteller. They watch the old man in anticipation, and his warm smile tells them tonight will be enjoyable and everyone will go from the warmth of the fire to their own homes with dreams of the ancestors and drumbeats of the elders as they sing, dance, sway, gesture and teach about the old ways.

All peoples of the world have legends of creation or special heroes that helped man establish his place among the creatures of the earth. Each is adapted to the environment that in turn helped create a unique culture. Percy Bigmouth's account is primarily a combination of his Lipan and Mescalero ancestry. It is lengthy, and some has been cut from the original manuscript to avoid repetition. Certain sections have had punctuation added or spelling changed for clarity. Sometimes, the past tense is not used at all. He used phrases like "someone suggest," "then they ask" or "he come up." Plurals are not always used either. However, for the most part, the material

Mountain Spirit Dancers. *Photo by Erik LeDuc.*

throughout these stories should always be viewed from the mind of Percy. His use of the semicolon and the comma instead of the standard period is unusual, but the reader will find this to be easy to follow after the first few paragraphs. Additionally, the sacred number four is often noted, and the characters are amazing in their diversity and personalities.

After reading a few of these tales, the reader will soon become enchanted by the Apache sense of humor, their reverence for certain figures and their colorful imaginations and descriptions of the world around them. Readers will also better understand the Apache mothers' dedication to raising their children. Much like Changing Woman, the Apache mother is a fierce champion for her children.

Most storytelling begins in winter months and with the legend of creation, moving on to other tales used to teach lessons or educate the listeners about the cultural mores of their society.

How All Creatures and Plants Came Out into the Wide World

Among us Lipans, our (creation) story goes like this:

So I'm here trying to write some more story about how the things start on this wide land.

They say in the beginning the people were down in the lower world, somewhere in the deep. There were all sorts of peoples, as I wrote before. They use one language. Then someone suggest to have a council, Then they ask, what the council about? Then someone said, Let's find another place to move. To where we move? You see there a light, above; suppose we send someone up there to find out about the upper world?

They just looked at each other, and ask who should be sent out up there. How about the wind? So they ask him, and the wind agreed to go up and see how it looked. He rose up. He is the whirlwind. He come up to the new world above. Nothing but water covered the earth. Then the wind start to get busy. He roll the water up like curtain. After the wind had rolled the water to its place, the upper world is ready for the people below.

Then they sent the raven up to look over the dry land. There are lot of dead fish and some other that live in the water. The raven never thought of going back down as he having a feast all by himself on these dead fish.

Then the people wondering, as the raven had said he come back and tell them about the upper world, But he never come back.

They look at the ceiling of the sky and see a little spot bright, very bright. It might be a hole in a star. And the people make a ladder; pretty hard, too high. Let's try hummingbird. He light and fast. They send him and he go round and round, up and up. Then he come back. "There is another place up there, but only water."

When the dry land appeared, It's all level all over. There were no mountains yet. The ground was just like ashes, some places kind of reddish spot, other places white with alkali surface. The people below wanted to hear the news, they waited but the raven never came.

So they held a council again to send someone. There are still some wide rivers, though they getting lower all the time. Then someone said, Let's send the Beaver out, so they sent the flat tailed Beaver. He too never come back, When he came up, the dry land and the clear river flowing; he is happy over the new world. He never thought of going back to tell the others. He started to get busy building dams. He went stream to stream. The people below wonder what had happen to the Beaver this time. Then they send the Gray Badger out, because the Raven and Beaver never come back to tell them what the place look like.

Then the Gray Badger go out, then back, He's faithful to his fellows who had sent him up. He go this way, and that way, all around. Most of the places are dried up, beautiful streams running, Then he went back to tell the other people. They all happy when the Badger got back and told them about the upper world. The Gray Badger is the only one who did the faithful work.

Now they send four fellow to look over the dry land. Again they had Mirage to fix the mountain and the hills. The clear brooks running down off the mountain and the foot of the hills, and they make little lightning, they make little arrows. That's the way it had been fixed up here on the earth.

Now all these were the people: Trees of all different kind, And little bushes of all sorts, The weeds of different kinds, Then animals of all sorts, And the fowls of all different kinds. They all happy, they all talk one language, even the rocks, and they all understand each other. They are the first peoples.

Then later the real humans came out after these animals and the trees and the plants: of course the different kinds of insects go out too. Now coming out and going around. These two are the leader, the Sun and the Moon, The sun is a man, and the moon is a woman. It's their ray, shine down on them; Both the sun and the moon. That's what these two meant, we be the leader. In the daytime, the sun show them their way to go, at night the moon. These two (Sun and Moon) said. We separate, but we will meet each other some time. That is when it eclipses, When they first come out they were going clockwise.

Then at last the others begin the start up, on the wide world they come up, coming out on their journey. The grey willow was first and said, I stop here and live, where nice little brook flowing. The grey willow stop first cause some of them got pretty old, so they stop there. Grey and green stand for old and young. They live together there. Then little later the alligator barked juniper stopped. He said, I stay here and live. He was wearing turquoise beads around his neck, which became his berries. Later on another of the juniper peoples stopped by. They too had turquoise beads, which they still wear. Then another juniper stopped next. They too wearing turquoise beads, it become his berries; There still another kind of juniper which stopped next. He was wearing reddish beads, and they became his berries also.

Next oak stopped. He was wearing black stones on his head. These are his acorns. Now as they went along another kind of oak stopped. He too wear black stones for his decoration, which became the acorns we gather today.

As they went along the choke cherry stopped. He has a red berries now, but it was red beads in those days. Then another tree stopped on the little hill, it was the mouldberry [sic] tree, He too wearing red beads, which become his berries now.

There was a river running southward. As the peoples were moving along, They never stop to sleep, just kept moving all the time. Then someone said sleep. So they stop at this place and they decided to sleep here. They wanted to move on, but someone put a white walking cane over them. Then they went to sleep. So one day and night had passed. Then the white streak linings on the eastern side. Someone said mornings. The Sun and Moon left them, and said to them, go ahead, nothing will disturb you people, They told their people to keep moving, no matter what happen on this earth. So the Sun become the War hero, Killer of Enemies. The Moon is Changing Woman!

Killer-of-Enemies when he left this world he gone back to the sun, that's where he is now! So the Changing Woman was living at this time: Here on earth yet, also there are several large Giant living around distant in different places: They begin eating people that come near their home. Of these Giant people are Big Owl, Antelope, Buffalo, Peccary, Flicker.

Now Changing Woman living at high mountain, They said she living at a place they call Rock nose. Indians name that; Now this mountain is standing just on the border of New Mexico though part in New Mexico But the Peak is in Texas.

Changing Woman Hides Her Son or Big Owl Threatens Thunder Son

The highest peak in Texas is Guadalupe Mountain. There a cave on the southeast side. (Also see Chapter 10: Son of the Rainstorm Hidden in a Cave.) That where the Changing Woman living when the earth is very young. But every time this Woman have a child, Big Owl came and eat the child.

The woman having a hard time trying to raise a child, the Big Owl come pretty often; But he don't bother the Woman; as this woman is sacred, only the child.

She wanted a child, so she went to a little spring, There she have contact with the dripping of the water. Then in a month she had the child. She called the baby, Child of the Water. He's a boy. Then Giant came; he thought he smell a baby; The woman said no! But he said yes, I smell the baby;

Well go ahead look for him, so the giant looked all around, but he can't find the child. Then he left. She change the child's name; she name him Hiding the Boy; because she had been hiding the little boy from the Giant. Later when the boy grow up to be a man, he had another name. At this time the giant had been busy trying to find the little boy; He come again, the little boy already walking around, soon the giant coming again; right away the little boy ran into his hiding place, The woman dug a hole under her fireplace. That where she hide her little boy. In four days this boy grew up to manhood. As the giant came, he looked around, he saw a baby foot track on the soft ground, Then the giant said, sure there must be a child somewhere, I saw his foot track, so he hunted around, but he never found the child. The woman had dug under the fire and kept a large flat rock. Then the Big Owl left, and the little boy came up.

He is big enough to shoot bow and arrow now, so the Woman made him a bow and arrow. The boy watched his mother. Then she said to her son: See this, She Had the bow in her left hand, then she made four arrow. Then she hold one in her right, put it on the bow and the string; teaching the boy how to handle the bow and arrow. Then the giant coming again. This time the little boy didn't run back in his hiding place. The Big Owl came, and he saw the boy. He said, "I want that little boy." He tried to think of some trick so that he could get the little child. But the mother spoke up. "I got the child from the water. So it's a Thunder child, I'm going to rear that boy for Thunder. You mustn't try to bother that child."

The Giant Owl went off, but he came back again. He's trying his best to get that child away from his mother. He couldn't persuade her to give him up.

Soon the boy learns how to handle his bow and arrow. The little boy is now into young manhood. He could take care of himself, anywhere. He had his bow and arrow, and could fight anything, He's pretty good shot with his bow and arrow, Then the Big Owl came again, but he didn't bother him; since the boy's Mother said, "My Child is a Thunder Son." Then the Big Owl afraid.

And that is legend of creation, of how we Apache come to this good earth.

Chapter 6

Its Strings Are Made of Rainbows

The Apache Cradleboard Ceremony

Good like long life it moves back and forth.
By means of White Water in a circle underneath, it is made.
By means of White Water spread on it, it is made.
By means of White Shell curved over it, it is made.
Lightning dances alongside it, they say.
By means of Lightning, it is fastened across.

Its strings are made of rainbows, they say.
Black Water Blanket is underneath to rest on:
White Water Blanket is underneath to rest on.
Good, like long life the cradle is made.
Sun, his chief rumbles inside, they say…
—From G. Goodwin's Social Organization of the Western Apache

I was warmed by the sun, rocked by the winds and sheltered by the trees as other
Indian babes. I can go everywhere with a good feeling.
—Geronimo (1829–1909)

When a child is born, it is a special event for all of us. Apache mothers were fierce guardians of their children, and when normal living in *rancherías* was a part of their world, Apaches also had another ceremony that today, while more rare in practice, is still indicative of some of the ancient beliefs that we can trace back to Child of the Water and his brave mother.

Child carried in old-style buckskin *tsach* (cradleboard), circa late 1800s.

One of the Apaches' favorite stories is about the beautiful cradleboard ceremony. It is often told during the Christmas season because it is similar to the story of the Christ child. Cradleboards continue to be used in many households, and the making of the cradleboard, or *tsach*, is special. The following account includes Eve's recounting of what Percy and Amelia

Naiche told her on several occasions. During these interview sessions, they often repeated what they had told before, but Eve never interrupted them because, as she told me, each time she would learn new details. This is not told in the vernacular of the Apache and has been written by the author based on these accounts.

———

When the Apache homeland is blanketed with snow, especially on the Sacred Mountain, Sierra Blanca, Christmas cannot be far, and with the advent of this extraordinary time, many people think about the Christ child and all that he represented. Among the Apaches, there is also great reverence and respect paid to Child of the Waters, born of White Painted Woman, these stories paralleling in several ways that of the Virgin Mary and her infant son. To honor children and Child of the Waters specifically, a beautiful ceremony that some traditional Apaches still adhere to, one that is poignant and indicative of the love and care given to the Apache child, is performed quietly, with dignity and respect for the ever-present rich heritage of the Apache. Some parts of the ceremony may have changed, but most have not.

The thoughts of every Apache mother when it came closer to the time of birthing might go like this: "My baby will be a strong one, that is for certain. I have chosen a *di yen* (person of strong character and ability) who can make a beautiful *tsach* for my child."

The selection of a *di yen* was extremely important for the family as well as the child. The *tsach* should be strong, crafted with care and blessed by the spirits, and it must fit the arms of the mother to be.

The thoughts of a *di yen* might be like this: "Though weary, I am very proud of my beautiful *tsach* and also of the healthy baby I have just finished placing within the buckskin padding. The child is now asleep, safe, warm and so beautiful. Her cradleboard will be the most important part of the child's life for many months. Yes, it has been a good day, and now it is time to rest…Now it is up to the family."

The Apache pampered and loved their children, as we all do. They treasured them not only as children but traditionally as part of a good economic future as well. Historically, mothers to be under normal situations—when war or running from the cavalry was not an everyday occurrence—were treated well during pregnancy, receiving special care, food and less of a work load. They did not ride or do heavy lifting or anything that might endanger the child.

However, the mother was required to do some work or else they believed she would develop lazy habits or pass them on to her child. The diet was also very precise: no meat with excessive fat or piñons. One had to be careful about bad spirits that always roamed throughout the region.

Of paramount importance were the selection of a talented cradleboard maker and the creation of the *tsach*. A woman was needed who could not only make a sturdy and beautiful cradleboard, but she must also be of good character who had lived a long and productive life. Certain individuals fitting these criteria within each band of Apaches, no matter what area of the Southwest, were known to the members of families expecting babies.

Among the Apache bands, differences in cradleboard styles existed but were minimal and often depended on regional resources. The cradleboard ceremony was also similar.

Four gifts usually sealed an agreement. Such gifts could be everything from *hoddentin* (sacred pollen and symbol of fertility) to a special knife, buckskin or calico, tobacco or metal cookware. In our modern world, a radio, TV, kitchen appliances or cellphones might supplement the more traditional gifts of the past century.

Prayers were always part of the ceremony. Construction was, and is, even today, a subject of great religious significance. Locating the proper materials for the *tsach*, the softness of the buckskin or canvas, the designs to be placed for good luck on the cradleboard—all were part of a multi-day process. It was best to have the *tsach* ready four days after the child was born.

Each *tsach* was measured carefully with the width at the center based on the measurement of the mother's arm from the elbow to her fist. This individual measurement made it more convenient to carry, hold or nurse her baby. The *tsach* protected children both physically and supernaturally. Prayers chanted during the construction of the cradleboard and the ceremony would have an effect on the child throughout its life. That is why its maker, construction and the design or use of good luck talismans were so important.

There were three main sections: the frame, the back slats and the hood or shade. Another part, a foot board made of ash, red cedar or oak, was moveable and could be lowered as the child grew.

For each section, a different plant was used. In some areas, the wood from the black locust was preferred. Other varieties of trees or branches could come from ash, oak or pine, although pine was usually not preferred as it attracted lightning. These woods were selected for the rounded frame. They were bent to an elongated loop, and the ends were carefully fastened to form the bed of the cradle. The back slats were often constructed of narrow leaf yucca if the child were to be a girl or *sotol* if a boy child. Padding made of rice grass and wild mustard and covered with soft buckskin or heavy canvas completed the major part of the *tsach*.

Next, the hood or "rainbow" provided a protecting arc over the baby's head, and should the cradleboard ever fall, the strength of that arc protected the child's head from damage. This was especially significant if it was a time of war. Women who did not have the baby attached to their backs in the *tsach* could grab the cradle on the run and suspend it on the saddle horn as they leapt into the saddle. Or the cradle could be hung from a tree branch, and the form would be strong enough to hold the weight of the child.

Beads or tiny bones when beads were unavailable were hung from the rainbow arc along with other good luck symbols. Colorful stones, shells, buckskin, feathers, sticks or wooden carvings were hung from the hood.

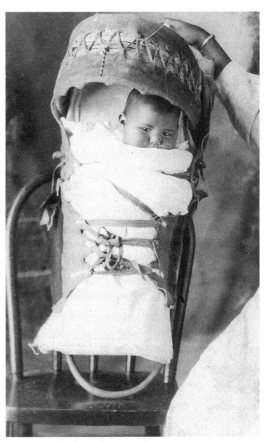

These provided items to amuse the baby, much like our mobiles hung over babies' beds today. On warm days, the buckskin flaps would remain unlaced so that either arms or legs could be free and kept cool. During cold winter months, a well-tanned bobcat skin or piece of fox fur might be used for warmth.

If the child were a girl, the buckskin laces were attached on the right side, or the left for a boy child. Designs of a half moon on the hood or arc would indicate a girl. Turkey wattle would have been included in a small pouch to protect a boy from lightning or the thunderbolts that often ripped open southwestern skies during summer's rainy season.

Cradleboard with child.

Some cradle makers placed small bags with pollen, lightning-etched wood to ward off lightning strikes or *cholla* wood to ward off illness, while hummingbird feathers and badger paws would prevent the child from being frightened.

Diapers of shredded cottonwood or juniper bark, moss or grass were used. Powder was made from ground willow bark and helped to keep the baby dry and comfortable. Apache mothers also realized that the baby's neck muscles had to develop, so for the first weeks, the cradleboard was kept in a horizontal position. After that, the vertical position on a mother's back, on horseback or leaning against a wall or tree was permissible.

Though confining, the cradleboard was the best way to keep the child out of harm's way, freeing the mother from the responsibility of constantly watching and fearing for her child's safety. Infants were held, rocked and fed while within its confines, usually from the time they were four days old until around one to one and a half years of age. Always, the baby was comfortable and well protected. To some, there was perhaps no more useful or special item devised for the care of an infant.

After birth, the new baby was rinsed in warm water, rubbed with a combination of fat or grease and red ochre and then quickly wrapped in a clean blanket or buckskin. This was accompanied by singing, prayers and sacred yellow pollen or ashes sprinkled to the four directions, and the midwife and other female relatives gathered around, each assisting the new mother. It was certainly a reassuring scene for the family. Mothers sang their own songs, but specific lullabies were relatively unknown, other than the cradleboard chants.

Oftentimes, if the baby was male, the umbilical cord was buried with special prayers among animal tracks. For example, if one wished his child to be a powerful warrior or leader, then it was buried among horse tracks; a great hunter would be buried among deer or elk tracks. Among the early Chiricahua and Mescalero, the umbilical cord was wrapped with buckskin and placed in branches of a fruit-bearing tree, thus allowing for that individual's life to be successful and completing the sacred circle of life.

In the past, the place of birth was also considered sacred. Geronimo, Daklugie, Chihuahua and Percy, as well as many others, spoke reverently of their birthplaces and remembered fondly how their parents returned to such locations. By rolling them in the sacred earth four times and holding them to the four directions, they renewed the child's good fortune. Unfortunately, hospitals have prevented this time-honored tradition.

Among some bands the ceremony had to be finished before noon. The cradle maker would hold the *tsach* to the four directions beginning with the east, toward the glowing warmth of the morning sun. Then clockwise, south, west and north. Gently taking the naked babe from the mother, the child was also held to the four directions. Warm water was rubbed on the child, and three times the baby was held toward the *tsach*. And on the fourth, the cradle maker placed the child within the cradleboard and the buckskin thongs were laced as prayers continued and sacred pollen was placed on both the mother's and baby's head and lips.

Afterward, everyone ate of special foods made from roasted mescal, ground acorn or mesquite beans, wild honey, yucca fruit and roasted haunches of venison or rabbit. Good-natured teasing, laughter and, of course, congratulations were offered to the new mother and, later, the father as well.

The warmth and strength of a cradleboard provided the infant with a sense of security, much as he had in the womb. And while to some life in a cradleboard may appear to be confining, we are told that the advantages far outweigh that factor.

If babies cried solely for attention, they soon found themselves taken from the familiar sights and sounds of camp and hung by the cradleboard in a tree. Eventually, crying ceased, which was critical during war time, during hunting forays or while trying to escape or hide from an enemy, because the crying baby was a dead giveaway, endangering the entire family or band. It should also be remembered that like all mothers, Apache mothers pampered, played and laughed with their children while making sure that diapers were changed and food given at proper times.

After several months, the child, being old enough to crawl, was allowed this

Apache mother and child secure in *tsach*, circa 1930.

freedom under the very watchful eye of everyone within the camp or home. Once the toddler began to walk, the *tsach* was, according to one Mescalero, placed in a pine tree, where it remained through rain, snow and sun. They selected a pine because of its long life and beautiful proportions, meaning hopefully that the child would also grown up tall and strong, much like this beautiful conifer. Others have noted that on occasion the cradleboard might be handed down to the next child, but a cradleboard ceremony was still held for each child. The more affluent would have a new *tsach* made so that each child would have its very own cradleboard and enter into the world in a manner fitting for all who love and respect their children and family traditions. Today, everyone has their own *tsach,* and that is as it should be.

"...Yes, it had been a good day, and now it was time to rest...
Good, like long life the cradle is made..."

Chapter 7

CLASSIC ANIMAL STORIES AND ANTICS

The protagonist of a folktale is always, and intensely, a young person moving through ordeals into adult life...
—Jill Paton Walsh

The following favorite tales encompass primarily animal stories and reveal how early Apaches shared the earth with their animal friends or enemies. We also have a new character, Raven Boy, entering the scene. Ravens are often found in Native American folklore. In this particular story, he is a helper and a brave warrior. Sometimes he is a valued counselor, sometimes a teacher and sometimes a rogue. He teaches Thunder Son many aspects of living in the new world they find awaiting them. One of the most important lessons is how to use the gift of the bow and arrow. Raven Boy teaches how to hunt and to take care of the animal once it is ready to become food for the people. We learn the process of "dressing" the deer, how to use the bow and arrow and how to pay respect to the animals that help us. An account of fire making is intriguing and descriptive as we learn of the *sotol* fire-making stick. We also see what happens during times of death, mourning and other cultural processes today as taught long ago by Raven Boy to Thunder Son, who passed on his knowledge, as any good teacher or leader would do.

A David and Goliath–style battle is included with the tale of the fearsome Giant Owl, often featured in stories of good and evil. Owls are looked upon in the Apache culture as loathsome creatures that bring only death and bad luck. If one dreams about an owl, it is believed to mean approaching death.

Adventures of Thunder Son and Raven Boy

Percy Bigmouth tried to capture this tale of Thunder Son for future generations.

Thunder Son's mother said, we need some meat; The boy asked what kind of meat; She said deer meat, so the boy got his bow and arrow. Went out toward the sun rise, the east. They say, as he started out, he call someone to go along with him. He called a Ravenboy. The Ravenboy came. Then they went on over the first little hill. On the eastern side they found their game, a big buck deer. The boy went and shot his arrow, hit the buck deer in back of the shoulder, in the heart. The deer made a few jumps and fell over. The boy went over, had his flint knife out, stuck it under the foreleg, to let the blood run out. Then the Ravenboy came over, and the hunter hand his flint knife to the Ravenboy, to dress the deer. He takes the skin off, cuts all the four legs off, and the ribs. Took all entrail out, clean out inside. Then the hunter cut pieces of the breast and cook it.

Then he start a fire with the *sotol* stick, by rubbing together. First he whittle the *sotol* to turn like a board, also whittle little *sotol* stick for the spindle, now he put his foot on the thin board like, put the spindle in his palm. He spin the stick, and soon the thin smoke curling up, few more stroke, the spark fell out, in the dry timber (tinder) under the fire stick. The Ravenboy pick the dry grass, and blew it. Soon it to blaze, put it down and start the fire. The Hunter set over there under the brush in the shade, watching the Raven. He's teaching how to do these things, and then the Hunter said to let the fire burn down to red hot coal, so it will cook the meat good. In the blazing fire, it won't taste right, only taste smoke. Then the Ravenboy took a stick to poke out the red hot coal. He put the meat over the red hot coal, and there they listening to the meat cooking, sizzling, The little breeze came toward with the smoke and fat. It sure smell good. Then he went to get the cooked meat.

But, Big problem—the Giant Owl saw the smoke of these two boys, and right away the Giant came on over and found the two Hunters; Just when the Ravenboy sat the meat before his Chief; the Giant Owl saw the fine meat, Giant Owl walk over to the meat, and said, "Ah! Is it for me to eat?"

With a loud heavy voice, He scared the Ravenboy, and the Giant pick the cooked meat up. The Ravenboy got so scared, he turn back, not watching. He's afraid to look at the big Giant, Then the Giant carry the cooked meat little way, sat it down before him. Ravenboy still facing the other way.

The Chief Thunder Son rising up and went over to the Giant, and say, "You said, we cooked it for you" but Then the Chief took the cooked meat up, and carry it back to where he was sitting. Just when the Chief sat down in good position, the Giant came over, pick the meat up, said the same thing, "It is it for me to eat" and he took it back to his place and sat down, The Chief went over and The boy took the meat and carried it back to his place. Four times they did the same thing on each side. Ravenboy trembling like he's freezing. This time Giant Owl got so mad he pull out his large bow and arrow, and went out in the open place, told the Hunter to come out and fight with bow and arrow. The young hunter went out too, had his bow and arrow out too, Then the fight start.

The Giant ask the boy to shoot first, but they said it was him the Giant to shoot, cause he's the one got mad first. So, the Giant aim at the boy, The arrow flew, The Thunder boy blow at the giant's arrow. It blow into splinter before it hit the boy; Then the boy shot and his arrow hit the giant, but the giant had some kind of armor. He had four layers on. When the arrow hit him, The first Armor came off. Again the Giant turn to shoot his second arrow, But his arrow didn't do any harm. The boy blew at the arrow as it came flying at him; It went to splinter again. The boy turn to shoot his Second arrow. It went flying and knocked the Second coat of armor. They did that four times on each side. The Giant tried to blow the boy's arrow, but no effect, Then the Giant says, How's that boy did that? I can't blow his arrow to pieces. Then Thunderboy shoot his last four arrows and hit the giant in his heart.

Then the Giant Owl says, when he felt the arrow, *awoh*! "You hurt me!" and staggering he fell over. The Ravenboy heard the voice of the Giant, he turn around saw the big fellow lying down. He walk to the Hunter, then they ate the meat. Thunder Son took extra meat back home to his Mother. Then she said, maybe there will be a people some day; so she got up, and look around, The Ravenboy went his way back to his camp, so today when someone go out hunting, the raven surely come along, to see if the hunter could get his deer, so he too can have what is left of the meat.

So, they say the Thunder Son gave a rule of the hunter to the Ravenboy to take care of the deer. When the hunter goes out, he, the Raven, must let the deer know that the hunter is coming. If he let the hunter have him, they must come out in the open place. If they refuse themselves to the hunter, they must stay out of sight, and don't let the hunter have a chance to get them. So today the raven always goes along, cawing to let the deer know to watch out. Yes I myself know this. I see the Raven and they sometimes give a hunter hard luck.

But at the same time The Thunder Son made a prayer for a hunter too: so the hunter say his prayer at night or early in the morning; and if the hunter sings this prayer well, the deer walk out in open grassy meadow. So that how the Indians hunt their game; though sometimes their prayer won't be answered. It is because they don't take care of the meat right when they bring it home. The wind is the messenger for the deer. The raven is helping the deer too; so that's the way its been fixed for the hunter.

Of course the White people don't believe in such a thing like that. It's a hard rule.

So that's that about the Thunderboy or Thunderson and the Ravenboy.

Raising of Little Deer

Percy had great respect for all animals. He told about the hunting of deer and antelope, describing in vivid detail how hunters disguised themselves and cleverly walked among a herd. This was done by many Native American groups, such as the Yaqui of Mexico, who are noted for their famous deer dancers, and also the Apache and Plains hunters. Sometimes they rubbed the scent of the animal on their bodies to disguise their own human odor.

Among the people, there are many hunting stories, and the following one related by Percy was one of Eve's favorites, as it included the bravery of a hunter and his reward for being clever and shows how even Apaches enjoyed the antics of the capricious fawn or, as Percy called them, "little deer."

Some people raising little deer or as you call, "fawn." In spring hunt deer and get little deer sometimes. People keep them around camp.

One time old couple told a person that came to visit that something was killing their little deer. They not know what or who was killing. They could not get close enough.

Antelope on the plains near Roswell.

One man say, "Look out at land; see that hill over there? Let's go there. We make noise and drive animals right past you. Then you kill."

They all got weapons, bow and arrow and lance, and went into the forest. They yell a lot and make big noise.

The man jump up on a big ledge. He has bow and arrow ready. All quiet.

Then he hears voices. Pretty soon he hear a noise in forest and something jump out at him! He shoot strong arrow. More noise comes out. Then he saw animal—big lion—with hair standing up on his back and its fangs show long and sharp. Lion makes jump at him but could not reach the ledge.

Brave man shoot lion in the throat and killed him.

This happen four times and every time he killed another animal who was killing the "little deer." The man and woman happy. They have pretty daughter and gave man daughter as his wife. The animals no longer came to attack the little deer. Everyone happy in camp.

Raven and the Owl and the Council of Death

It should be noted that very few times is death discussed in this way, especially in the old times.

Now here I'm going to try, to write about the birds and animals having a meeting about death. So one day they gather together, Then the argue started, The raven came in last. He asked what the meeting about, Some one said its about death and how to get person back. So we ask you to be our leader now, and judge these questions; This is what we want to do, When a person die, lets get him back in four days, We wanted it that way, No let him be gone forever, not to come back to life; How you think raven; The raven said No, not a good idea.

But then in a few days, somehow the raven lost one of his children. The people scatter all around, Then someone said, raven lost a child, Then the raven going around and got all the people together, and said to them, you people had an argument several days ago, You people want the dead to come back to life in four days. Now my child died, so I want it your way.

No, you have already said let them be gone forever, you the one that rule that way. We asked you the very first, but you wanted death forever, so now we stay on the rule.

Then raven started to cry, tore his clothes away and cut his hair, Then went out half naked. So now the Indian people follow that rule, when someone lost in the family. Throw their things away, cut hair; And then the owl come to the raven and said to him, you look poor, but its your own fault, you the one made the rule, so now you ragged, and the other people told him the same thing. There is no use for you to cry: The owl says, I'll bury the body, and I'll take care of the body after death.

The raven angry, then said, When the cold weather come again, We'll have a meeting, just between you and myself; Alright said the Owl, we'll fix it in an easy way, The owl said again to the raven, you had spoiled all the plan which the people had wanted. Also you left your child right in the open place, where you thought you could see the body all the time, So I'm going to bury it.

Again the raven said, We'll meet again about this when the cold weather come.

I don't care said the owl. Then later the cold weather come, The Raven went looking for the owl. The raven said, "Some time while back we had said we meet again, so today is the day, It this way, suppose we sit up there on the limb where the cold wind cut you through, The owl said, I've already said, I don't care what becomes of me; and I still had that in my mind; The raven said, lets see who will be tough: and could stand through this cold night,

So they set side by side on the limb. Then way in the night, the raven asked the owl, how does it feel, the owl said not so cold, then later the raven asked the owl again, This time the owl said, I feel little chilly through my feather. Then the raven said I'm just shaking my feather out. Then later toward the morning the owl said whoah, I'm beginning to freeze. Raven said I'm just fluttering my feather and not so cold, little later the owl said, he about to drop off.

Raven said you are no owl. The sun strike the hill above, then the owl drop off and died, The raven came down, and pick the owl up, and said to the dead body of the owl, "you are not much of a bird, froze to death,"

The raven throw the owl between rock; and told the owl you better find a warmer place next time. The raven talking to the dead body of the owl. Said the raven to the owl, you had said you can out stand me in the cold, but you had found it out, that the raven is much tougher!

Though Raven won the contest, his son never came back to life. Of course, the rule was never changed and today people do not come back to life as agreed upon by the Council. However, we see reasons why, at least according to legend, that the Apaches like many other Native Americans and Hispanics, have their own way of expressing grief. In addition to wailing and cutting off their hair as noted in this story, some also used to cut off a finger as a deep sign of mourning.

In the past, the personal items were either buried with the deceased, or burned. Livestock such as a favorite horse or cattle were shot.

The owl is also feared by the Apache (and Navajo) as he is the one, as shown here, who comes for the spirit of the departed or is the harbinger of death.

Death customs have changed in some ways among the majority of Apaches since the early part of the twentieth century. Nevertheless, certain features of earlier periods prevail. No one who attends such a funeral today can ever forget the keening and death wail with its haunting, tragic sound.

The Foolish People

Every culture has them. So, too, do the Apaches. Percy told Eve once about these individuals. One would imagine no one would want to have much contact with such imprudent or childish actions.

Now here a story about what we [the Apaches] call "foolish people" who lived nearby. A Mescalero man was married to one of these foolish people so he had to live with his wife's band. These people did not wear many clothes, nor have houses. They had no horses and when they found a horse they had no idea what to do with the animal. They not know how to get on a horse either so they say.

One day this Mescalero brought his horse to the camp of these people. No one knew what to feed him. They did not know what to call him. The people called council to discuss. Some people tried to feed him white gravy. Horse not like it at all. Then they tried coffee. The horse did not like either. They tried mescal, and venison, and all other food in camp. That Mescalero warrior laugh and laugh. Finally he took his horse to grassy area and the horse ate and ate. The foolish ones cried out, "Look, he must like grass."

Then everyone wanted to ride the horse. One got on but faced the back. Another tried and fell off. Finally that Mescalero got on right and rode around all over. He loped and ran horse and the foolish people said that Mescalero man must have put pine pitch on his back side to keep him on right.

Two Foolish Men Escape Comanches

Comanches are in so many of the Apache stories. The following is humorous and not of the usual fighting mode.

Two men had made a fire and were cooking rabbit for dinner. Some enemy people, the Comanche, were coming from the Plains and sneak up on Foolish men. They were going to kill them. One of mens throw part of rabbit gut over shoulder into bushes and hit a Comanche. The Comanche thought that was such a foolish thing to do that he began to laugh and gave away their hiding place. So the two Foolish mens get away from there fast. They say they ran fast. They say that these foolish people run very fast, faster than horses so soldiers and enemies hardly ever catch them. Cowboys can't catch them either.

Turtles Go Raiding

These were the only "Foolish People Stories" Percy talked about. Mostly he thought they were, well, "foolish." Another humorous tale is about turtles and how they decided to go on a raid. As Percy says, this one is a warning to children not to grow up and become adults like these turtles.

Will now try to write about some Turtles who go out raiding. Now this story shows how some people were in the old days and it was a warning to the children not to grow up like the turtles. They talked big but they never did much against the enemy. The people knew they were big liars and had no respect for them.

The Turtles had been just sitting around camp when one of them said, let's be mens, not to hang around the camp all the day long. Let's go out and raid. So they went out scouting. They went along. They came to a canyon where a big tree had fallen across the trail. They tried to go to the other side of it. One would crawl up and fall back, and then another. They worked at it all day long but had no luck. Finally they were all tired out.

They all said, "Let's go back home and tell the others we had a big fight anyway." So the turtles returned but the people in camp were surprised. "Why here those fellows came back without horses, and without even one scratch or wound. They have not lost a man."

The turtles replied, "Oh, we had a great fight. You should have been there. We got many horses. The enemy did not see us take them and we were well on our way before a big crowd of them discovered it and came after us and circled us. We had to let horses go, but we had great fight with the enemy even though we not get even a scratch or lose a man. You should have seen it, the fight. We got away and made for the hills!"

Chapter 8

OLD COYOTE (THE TRICKSTER) TALES

Coyote is always out there waiting, and coyote is hungry.
—Native American proverb

Coyote talked to the trees, even to the rock and water. But all the time he play a mean trick on his friends…in return he always get the worse back on him…all this happen when old coyote speaking like a human.
—Percy Bigmouth

As we have seen, every tribe has legends similar to those of Reynard the Fox or old Br'er Rabbit. In these, as in some of the badger stories, someone is shrewd, cunning or unscrupulous or sometimes a combination of all three. It varies with the tribe. Some have the wolf, others the bear, lion or coyote. There are other animals used in this capacity as well.

In a talk before a local historical society in El Paso, Dr. C.L. Sonnichsen once described the Coyote stories as practical institutions for the young. Coyote was the personification of antisocial habits—a trickster and a low fellow who got into difficulties and made himself a laughingstock because he did not behave as a decent or correct Apache should.

However, Coyote was really much more than a trickster, as we shall see in the following pages revealing both the good and mischievous side of this unique character. As modern or even as primitive teaching tools, these stories were often very effective in making people take notice and learn from these all-too-human errors presented by Coyote. He reminds us that there are unintended consequences, and we must learn from our mistakes. By learning, we are freed from life's traps.

Other questions one should ask when discussing Coyote might be: Was Coyote like he is today, or did he look like a man? Did Coyote or other animals wear clothing like the Apache? Did they walk on all fours? Coyote could be good and bad, much like people are today. He helped people to obtain fire, food or the "fat," but then he played tricks on his friends so that he would come out ahead of everyone. However, he often got paid back for this mischief. Other times, his bad behavior banned him from a village, much as some people tend to be avoided today.

When one hears Coyote howl, we know he is acting foolish or crying out because he got hurt by his childish antics. However, when he is on the hunt, he is always depicted as smart or cunning. He taught the Apaches how to gather mescal, a staple of their diet of old. We also learn that because Coyote tried to steal fire from the sun to help man, he ended up with a dark streak at the end of his tail. His tail got singed when he got too close to Father Sun. Although he was trying to be helpful, he was also caught in the act of stealing from the sun.

Old Coyote howling. *Illustration by Gary Stilwell, Lincoln, New Mexico.*

The following are from Percy's written tales and/or interviews with Eve. They have been rearranged slightly for better understanding of the reader. As Percy wrote to Gene, "Hope my friends enjoy my Coyote stories. Which I had wrote, as I did the best I can. But don't mind my error, Correct them, as you go through the story."

Coyote and the Red Ant People

This time on his journey, Coyote visit the Red Ant People. On trail at the foot of a hill there was big camp; As coyote was coming out on the flat he hear big noise coming from the hill; he stop to listen, then he go on. Soon he could hear people talking and laughing...Se-wa-ah-ha.

Coyote love to have good time. He came closer; someone whisper, "There comes coyote. Sing good and loud." They watch him from the bottom of the teepee, but he does not see them.

Then Coyote come and peep inside; he saw only one big woman cleaning up. Coyote was puzzled. He know he heard many people talking and laughing. He want to have fun too. Now he see no one but big woman. Then he started to walk away; but then Ant people start to sing. Coyote sneak up again but the noise stopped. When he came near, the Ant people run for their hole in earth. Still he saw only the big woman busy shaking the rug. Coyote didn't know this lady was their leader.

While he was peeping inside some of the Red Ant Boys went outside behind him. Then all the rest came out to sing. They invite Coyote to come in. Just then the Red Ant Boys from outside push Coyote into teepee and cover the entrance; rest of Ant Boys jump on him. Coyote jump this way and that way. He brush off Ant Boys, but there are too many. Finally they open the door of teepee and Coyote jump outside and run away. He hurt bad from all those bites.

Coyote and the Arrow People

Now, here I write a story about Coyote visiting the Arrow People. After he visit the Ant people he go along and find a teepee with many arrows. Many fine arrows feathered with the eagle feather. Only one had a turkey feather and it was a poor arrow. When mens come they take good feathered arrows to hunt buffalo. Coyote end up with poor arrow. All mens get their Buffalo, even Coyote with bad arrow. All men bring in the entrails and put near fire and then returned the arrows to their places.

When the people ate up all their buffalo meat, they come in for the arrow once again as someone say the Buffalo are coming. They get arrows with eagle feathers and Coyote does the same. All mens get their buffalo and so does Coyote even with the bad arrow. But he does not bring in the entrails, nor does he return the arrow. He was ashamed to use it while the others had fine arrows. He had four of those poor arrows. He became angry. Then he shot at a rock and shattered all four of them. Then he broke his bow. He came in. The others once again brought entrails to the teepee. He did not. Others brought their bows and arrows back but Coyote left his broken at the hunting grounds.

That night the broken arrows and bow return by themselves to the teepee of the Arrow People. Next day mens go out hunting again only this time Coyote go inside and takes the best arrow and bow. He gets his Buffalo too but never returns to that camp. He takes everything on his way. He left the arrow people.

Now, today, sometime the people borrow something from their friends, they don't bring it back, and some of them are not honest with their friends, Of course Coyote had started that liar, crooked business.

That way some people are today, so that the end of our bow and arrows story.

Wildcat Teaches Coyote a Lesson

Here another story. It started like this. Coyote went to visit Wildcat, Coyote said, let's have some fun, Wildcat said what will be the game, as Wildcat was lying down, and also Coyote was lying down. Coyote looked at Wildcat's paw, and he reached for it. You've got a very fine soft paw he said. He began to lift it up. He got hold of the wrist, He put Wildcats paw on his face, It is soft and he said. Look at mine. It is rough and hard. Suppose we scratch each other? Wildcat said no I don't want to do that, you said that because you've long nails, like to get the best of me.

But Coyote kept asking and Wildcat finally agreed. Where will we start. On the wrist? He asked. No. on the back, decided Coyote. You scratch me first said the coyote. No said, the Wildcat, you do it first. They argued about it. Finally Wildcat persuaded Coyote to do it first and lay down, Coyote scratched him. While he did it Wildcat squirmed and said, ah! Ah! He made believe it hurt, but it wasn't much because just a little fur come out and the scratch wasn't deep.

Then Coyote lay down, Wildcat stood over him and shot his claws out. He sank them into coyote's back and brought them downward. He pulled off the flesh and the fur as he raked Coyote's back.

Coyote had been fooled. Coyote groaned, Wildcat put the fur skin and flesh in front of him. The claws were back again. Coyote couldn't understand it. He said, I don't see any claws, you must have used something sharp on me. No, look, said Wildcat, and he shot out his claws. Then Coyote knew.

That is why many people get fooled today, and some are smart and can do things but don't show off. But when they have to do something, they come out best and fool the others like old Wildcat.

Coyote and Prairie Dogs

On his way back home old Coyote found the feather of a red tail hawk. Since Coyote was close to Prairie Dog town he thought of a trick he would play.

One of the Prairie Dogs saw him coming and sounded the alarm. But old Coyote he say, "I have some good news for you people. See, I have killed your enemy." And he showed them the red tail hawk's feather.

Finally all the prairie dogs believed him and came out of their holes.

Coyote then suggested they stop up their holes and have a big celebration, an enemy scalp dance.

So, they had big dance and feast. Coyote say he want all the big fat fellers to dance on the inner circle and that he would be their leader. While they were singing and dancing Coyote struck one on head. Then he told the others that that fellow was so happy with his dancing that his heart burst. Two more fell the same way.

At last one old Prairie Dog Woman and her grandchild saw what Coyote was up to. She shouted in alarm but no one would believe her. Then, at last another one saw Coyote hit his friends on head with big rock. All the Prairie Dogs believed the old Woman now and ran for their holes.

But they all covered up! As they fought to get them re-opened throwing the dirt aside and trying to get in, Old Coyote came along and hit each on head with rock.

At last he gathered all the Prairie Dogs and carried them to the edge of the forest where he had a great heap of burning coals. He opened it up and put all the fat Prairie Dogs inside. He could hardly wait.

But Coyote very sleepy now after all the dancing so he take a nap while the prairie dogs were roasting.

Why Coyote Looks the Way He Does

Now, while Coyote was waiting for those Prairie Dogs to roast he takes a nap.

As he slept, along came Bobcat who being very clever found all the delicious food in the fire. He made a feast all by himself and ate them all but the old grandmother and her grandchild. He then put them and the bones of the others back in the fire.

"Now, I am going to play another trick on Coyote." Bobcat pulled the Coyote's ears straight up, his tail out and then pulled his nose out and squeezed his paws together. He stretched his back bone. That made him look funny. Then Bobcat left.

When Coyote wake up he feel funny all over. "My face feel different!" he shouted. He began to feel his face, as one will do when one gets up early in the morning and rubs his eyes, Oh he said, my face feel funny, like been stretching. It's long, he stretch himself, my body feels different, His ears were long and pointed. He ran to the water and saw his reflection. He couldn't believe how he looked. He sat on the bank and looked at his reflection in the water.

Then he remembered his feast and ran back to the fire since he was very hungry now. But only bones and the old lady prairie dog and her grandchild were there.

They not fit to eat he groaned and flung them into a tree. Disgusted he went back to look at his reflection and saw the two prairie dogs' reflections instead. But he did not know they were up in tree, he thought they were in the water and coyote jumped in after them.

Coyote was really hungry, confused and angry. He dove into water again and again and then he tired out.

Bobcat did this to me he decided. I'll fix him! Old Coyote now thinking of revenge and he goes on his way.

Why Bobcat Looks the Way He Does

Coyote found Bobcat asleep. He remember the prairie dog feast that Bobcat cheated him out of. Now is time for revenge. He made medicine over sleeping Bobcat and then pushed his long tail in and shorten his body, his fingers and his head. Satisfied with his work he went off to his home.

But, Coyote's children were afraid of him. He tried to call them but they thought he was a stranger. He called them by name and told what had happened. Then they believed him.

In the meantime Bobcat woke up and felt very strange. He, too, realized that his body was changed and he knew who had done it to him. He goes home to his children and they too were afraid of him until they finally understood.

And that is why Coyote and Bobcat look like they do today and why they don't like each other. They avoid each other.

Coyote and Rabbits

Now here another story about Coyote with the Rabbit: The rabbit play sick and got away from the Coyote; It happen this way, Coyote went along on the trail, he happen to see cottontail on the trail. The rabbit saw that he had no way of escape from the coyote, So the rabbit throw himself by the trail, as the coyote come up to the rabbit. Coyote said Ah! How are you going to get away from me, But the rabbit lying underneath of little bush, and just few yard away, Where the rabbit had his hole. Then the rabbit said. Oh don't bother me; I'm sick said he: Then the Coyote asking what's the matter? Again the rabbit said he's sick: Then he told the Coyote that he was coming to see him; to see if you got some medicine, The rabbit grunted and grunted, Then he threw out little bit of excrement from his hind end, only a very little came out. That's the trouble with me, he told the coyote. My bowels won't move, I'm having a hard time for a whole day: Then the coyote said. I can cure that, he looked around for medicine. But he wouldn't go far, and the rabbit just kept wishing to see the coyote head turn, But coyote kept his eye on him all the time: Finally Coyote reach for a stick to dig, Then that rabbit got away and into his hole.

That's the first story.

Here another story but, it tell different way, some part are the same, Just to have some fun over the Coyote story: Well it start like this: Some people were coming on the path, On ahead of them, saw the coyote was coming toward them, So they took the rabbit skin: and put some rock in it. Then they put it under the brush: Coyote came along, he looked at it sideways. He made believe he didn't see it and was going to pass by. But he was watching it out of the corner of his eye. When he got opposite it he suddenly jumped at it, put his paw down, and bit at it. Ah! He said. My teeth pain me, I ache all over. He got away from there. He went on a little way. He saw another rabbit. Oh I'm not going to go after that one; he said its nothing but rock rabbit. He wouldn't go after it. This rabbit was a real one and kicked up the dust and ran away. Coyote was very angry.

Coyote went along. He come to another rabbit. I wasn't think it's a rock rabbit this time; he said. He made believe he was going to pass by, but then he jumped at it and put his paw on it. It was a real rabbit. He bit at it a little, being careful this time. The rabbit played dead and coyote thought he had it for sure. The rabbit was caught under a bush. Coyote was talking to himself. I won't let it go this time, he said. This is how I did it, He backed off from the rabbit and jumped at it and put his paw on it again. I'll do it again. He backed off again and jumped at it again. The brush was sticking out on top over the coyote. Coyote jumped higher and the brush hit him in the eye. His eye hurt and he held it. While he had his eye covered, the rabbit saw his chance and ran away, So Coyote lost his rabbit again: Then he went along, Another rabbit was sitting there. Before coyote got near, The rabbit ran off, Coyote chased him. Just as coyote was about to catch him, the rabbit darted in a hole. Coyote peeped in there. He saw something at the bottom, He reached in. He could just about touch the fur of the rabbit. Coyote said, I'm going to get you pretty soon.

They say He dug to enlarge the hole and tried again He couldn't quite reach the rabbit anyway. He had to give up, and went on his way but was very hungry. And that story of Coyote and rabbits.

How Fat Skull Women Escape Old Coyote

Today I write story, short version, about Fat Skull Women and how they escape from Coyote.

Now Old Coyote going on his way but he getting hungry. He know of camp of Fat Skull people. They fat and Coyote bring them deer to eat four times. Coyote go off on journey, but then get hungry. He getting closer to their camp now. He's going pretty fast, he's getting near to the women, and thinking of good meal. The women see him and run. Coyote run faster. Women run over river and rocks.

Just then the women come to a cactus. They gather some cactus and scattered on behind them so the coyote can't travel fast. Coyote come to the place where the Fat Skull scattered the cactus, He having a hard time to pass, finally he got by, so he start after them again. These three Fat Skull women come to a wide water, that is a river. They didn't know how to get across, Just then a Crane happened to be there at the bank, so they asked the crane. "Could you help us get across," so Crane put his leg across and they used it for a bridge. When they got on the other side, one of the women stretched her hand wide and made the water ever wider so that coyote couldn't get over; Then Coyote came, He tracked them but pretty soon he get tired and forget about it.

So, that is how the three Fat Skull women escape. Now these three women are the insects we call potato bugs, red spotted insect; and the pretty red bird. Sometimes people change names to stay safe or begin in new home.

Coyote and Bear

Fat, suet, bear grease or any animal fat, entrails or organs were held in high esteem by numerous peoples throughout the world, especially during the cold winter months. They believed that when prepared with nuts, berries or dried meats, these products were a way to ward off the cold and, of course, hunger that comes with lean winter months and very little meat. Prepared like this it was quite tasty. Additionally, fat was used to prepare hides and maintain the suppleness of buckskin.

Well, here goes the story about the Coyote visiting the camp where the Bear is chief. At this camp no one is supposed to keep the FAT when they kill game. Bear Chief wanted it all! Every day he would send his two Bear Boys out among the people of the camp and they gave them all of the fat.

One day Coyote came to visit camp; he looked it over. He liked what he saw and he decided to bring his own camp over.

Then one of the peoples came to his camp and asked him if he knew the rules of their camp? Coyote said no. Well, said the visitor, in this whole camp no one is supposed to keep the fat of any kind. That was the way of their Bear Chief.

Old Coyote say, "I am not going to give any fat to your Chief if *I* kill the game."

The visitor said, "You better or he will come and punish you." Coyote was angry and the visitor returned to his own camp.

Next day Coyote go hunting; he killed nice fat young buck. As Coyote brought the deer in right away the Bear Chief saw him and sent his two Bear Boys to get the fat.

When Boys arrive Coyote step out of his teepee and ask them what they want.

"We came after the fat, ALL of it from that deer you brought in."

No said Coyote.

One of the Bear Boys said, "Our Papa is chief here. We are not going until you give us that fat!"

"I say no, You two boys go home."

Bear Boys not go, and keep asking for the Fat; Coyote get a stick and gave Bear Boys a good whipping. They both start to cry and return to camp of Bear Chief.

Old Coyote pretty smart. He know that the Bear Chief would come for a visit soon so he start to build a big fire and around the fire he scattered some pieces of deerskin large enough to cover the palm of hand. Also he put some pebbles in the fire.

When the Bear Boys returned their Papa asked them why they come back without any fat and why they crying.

"That new camper down there, He is the cause of all of this."

Now Papa Bear is mad and he goes down to the Coyote camp. Coyote has his big fire going and all of the people go down to see what will happen.

Bear Chief came growling and said he was coming after the fat. Coyote say no, "this fat belong to me because I was the one who killed the deer and brought it in."

Bear Chief angry. He say, "You whip my two boys too, so, first I finish with you, then I take the fat!"

Now, old Coyote can be brave. He stood his ground by the hot fire. The Bear Chief starts around this way, and then Coyote runs on the other side. They both circle the fire. Then Coyote say to Bear, "I am not afraid of you either. Open your big mouth a little wider. It won't frighten me!"

Coyote kept saying that while he picked up the hot pebbles with one of the pieces of deer skin that he had put near the fire. Then he throw it into Bear's mouth. Bear Chief very angry and he not notice that the hot pebbles were thrown in his mouth. He continue the chase.

Coyote did the same thing number of times. Pretty soon the hot pebbles began to take affect and Bear Chief drop dead.

Now, the Mother Bear had come down to see for herself why the Father Bear did not come back. There she saw the Bear Chief laying dead. Then she is sad and very angry too. She went after Coyote and Coyote circle around and do the same thing with Mother Bear. He race around the fire faster making fun of Old Mother Bear. He mocked her. Soon old Mother Bear drop dead too.

Old Coyote the hero now. He killed both of the bears. He won the fight and he also won the fat back for the whole camp. Everyone is happy and they have a big feast. Now they could eat all the fat they wanted. No one would ever again try to take all of the fat. And the two sad Bear Boys had to make their own living, hunting the food for themselves.

How Coyote Stole Hawk Chief's Wife

We see some interesting relationships within this folk tale, and we learn again that Coyote can be good but devious in his mischievous shenanigans. The tongue of an animal is considered by many to be a delicacy, just as was the "fat" in the previous Coyote story. We also find out why Bat hangs upside down. This is one of the few times we see Bat emerge in an Apache folk tale as a character. (Also see chapter 10 on caves and bats.) Other lessons show how people can turn on their leader, but sometimes it can also backfire.

Old Coyote always been visiting. This time he visits Hawk Chief's camp where the people cannot keep the good tongue when they bring in their game. Coyote come to stay and he brings his son.

Now the Hawk Chief had a son too, and also his wife is very beautiful.

Hawk Chief send warrior to visit Coyote's camp; and to say that in this camp the people don't eat the tongue.

Coyote ask why and say that tongue is finest part of deer or other animal to eat.

Well, old Coyote don't like this at all and say, "Come, you mens, let us hold council about that Hawk Chief."

Everyone comes and they ask at council what could be done. Some also ask Bat for his advice.

At first Coyote tells the people they have to dig a big trench. They all ask the Bat if it is a good idea and he tells them to do what Coyote says.

Then they build a big fire. They made it red hot and cover the top over with branches.

Then they call their chief. Hawk Chief arrived with his war club, bow and arrow. He never was without them. The people had prepared a fine place for him but when he started to sit down he fell into the trench!

For a long time the people had tried to get rid of their chief because they all wanted to eat tongue. When he fell in the pit they rushed over and covered him up with the hot coals. He died in that way.

Some time before this happen the people had said whoever got rid of their chief could have the chief's wife as a gift; Coyote took the Hawk Chief's wife for he was the one who gave advice that lead to his death. Next day everyone moves camp.

Now Hawk Chief had a brother, another hawk; this brother crying around the old camp while the remainder of people moved away. He mourned his brother and said he would wait for him to come back. At last he heard a tiny voice that said; you been crying too much. You have troubled us a lot and keep my children awake. I don't have chance to sleep. What is the matter?

The voice came from the ground, it was the ground squirrel. Hawk could not see who that person was. The voice called him again. What is the trouble?

Then he explained that just four days ago they called my brother to his terrible death.

All right say Ground Squirrel. You go over to that camp; dig around and look for any remains. It does not matter if you find only a small charred piece of bone. Get it and bring it here.

Hawk did so and found some burned pieces of bone. Ground Squirrel said, make a little nest on that tree limb. Put that charred bone in there; make the nest strong so it won't fall off. Each day for four days look in the nest.

Hawk did as he was told and on the fourth day he found one egg! The next day he found that egg had hatched and a tiny red being was in there. He looked again on the fourth day. The bird already had fluffy feathers. It was his brother!

The next day he visited his brother and he had his war club, bow and arrows. Hawk Chief asked the Ground Squirrel where his camp had moved. He was told that they had dragged their moccasin strings in a certain direction.

He started after them with revenge in his heart.

On the way he find a teepee peg and asked Peg, How long has it been since they passed through here? Peg reply, they drag their moccasin strings through here four days ago.

Hawk Chief continues after them. He found another peg; He asked, You Who Get Pounded on the top of the Head, how long has it been since they passed through here?

Maybe four days ago say Peg.

He went along following their movements and was told the people had been there little while ago and the camp is just over the ridge.

Hawk Chief climb the ridge and saw his family. His wife was carrying a heavy pack and holding their son's hand.

The chief shot an arrow far ahead of them. When they came to the arrow, the little boy reached out and exclaimed, this my father's arrow.

The mother reply, No do not say that. They killed your father and no one must speak of him anymore. We must forget him; we not look back.

Even when they see this arrow sticking in the ground they did not look back. Hawk Chief shoot another arrow. And another and yet a fourth one.

His son say, "I carry these arrows along. I may use them some day."

Hawk Chief threw his bow ahead of them. Their reaction was the same. He threw his war club ahead of them. They never looked back, that is the rule. One does not look back when they are leaving the dead.

Finally, as a last chance the Chief threw all of his possessions ahead of them and said, Shoooo!

They turned and stared. The woman saw her former husband; they cried because they were so happy to see each other; they sat and talked. Hawk wanted to be hidden so he could get revenge on Coyote. His wife hid him in her quiver. At sunrise she caught up with the people of her band. She used to be a beautiful woman but Coyote was jealous so he had pulled out most of her hair and treated her mean.

Coyote had gone out hunting and at sundown he returned calling for his wife. Aho, my wife, what is the matter? Why don't you come out to help me bring in this meat? He called her in this way four times.

Hawk Chief told his wife from his hiding place, Don't go out to that Coyote. Make him carry it in himself. So Coyote bring that deer in and threw it down. The Woman picked a good piece and started to prepare it saying, I am going to fix this for my husband. She boiled it in the clay pot. Then she said; I have boiled the meat for my husband.

Coyote thought that she meant it was for him so he was happy when she said "husband." But he find out that not true! Hawk Chief had returned and wanted revenge.

Now you know that the people in this band had been eating the tongue since the death of their Hawk Chief. Coyote was the one who gave them back this right. But now the Hawk Chief gave orders to Coyote to go out and get the tongue.

Why the people ask; you told us we could eat the tongue now.

Coyote said yes, but that Hawk Chief was now going to get all of the tongue! And he took the tongue to Hawk Chief's camp.

Hawk Chief's Revenge on Coyote and Bat

Next morning, the Hawk Chief told Coyote that by the old juniper he should build a fire and after that call all of the people to come for a big council. Then Hawk Chief asked, Which of you men advised that my wife be given away? And that I be killed?

Coyote, trying to cover for himself, whispered, "The Bat." But others told the chief that it was both Coyote and the Bat.

All right, Coyote, you go out and find four rocks. Put them in the fire. Coyote did so. Then the chief told him to go and get the fat that covers the deer stomach. The Chief took out one hot rock and wrapped fat over the rock. He made Coyote swallow it.

Coyote moaned. This is bad thing you do; but he swallow it anyway. He had to swallow the others too. At the fourth one he rolled over dead.

Hawk Chief was also very angry at the bat. He turned to the bat. Bat got his punishment when the Chief grabbed him by the legs. The juniper tree was standing there, and the Chief threw Bat up in the tree. He had long moccasins, and they caught on the limb. He hung there head down. He could not escape. And that is why Bat hangs that way today, even when he is asleep his head is downward.

And that is our Lipan story of how Coyote stole the Hawk Chief's pretty wife and how Hawk Chief got his revenge.

Chapter 9

OF DOVES AND OLD BROWN TURKEY

There is a road in the hearts of all of us, hidden and seldom traveled which leads to an unknown, secret place.
—*Chief Luther Standing Bear*

After the flood, as humans spread out they carried with them stories of the flood, passed down over generations. Each civilization began to include their own ideas about the story…subtle changes made were to reflect the culture and religion of their world, yet always they retain certain basics to what might have occurred.
—*Lynda Sánchez*

The next two tales are unique, especially the first one about San Hilando. No one can explain if this is an Apache or Spanish term although it sounds like it could be of Spanish origin. We have placed these two tales together because they specifically talk about birds: doves and turkeys. The first about Dove Girl came from the Big Chief tablets used by Percy and sent to Gene, and the second is from interviews with Percy by Eve Ball. The first is no doubt more in the tradition of the Lipan side of Percy's family and describes a special secret place. It could have been added to the folklore repertoire before the Lipans' arrival at Mescalero. The story of old brown turkey is about the Great Flood, and almost every tribe in the world interestingly has such a tale of flooding and destruction of their known world.

The Clever Young Man and Dove Girl (In Search of San Hilando)

A young man of the Lipan started out toward the east and came out on the plains. There he met three men. One wore a gray hat, another special leggings and the third one had a cane. As the young man came up to them, the one with the hat say, "This hat, when someone wears it, nobody can see him."

The second man say, "When someone wears these leggings, nobody can outrun him."

The third man say, "With this cane, you can carry heavy load long distance, even if you are old man."

Now, the young man became interested when he heard all of this. He listened some more.

"Now, here is what we are trying to do. We want only one person to take care of these objects. We trying to figure out who among us should do so. Can you figure out who it should be?" they asked the young man.

"That is easy. See, there is nice open lane. All three of you walk down there and from that place race back here. Whoever comes back here first shall take care of all three items."

Believing young man is wise, the mens begin the race. As soon as they leave the young feller put on gray hat and walk off toward the east. He also put on leggings and take the cane. All this happen while the three old mens racing one another. When they come back to where young man supposed to be, he gone. The clever young man gone. They never see him again.

This smart young man continued his journey until he came to a pretty spot. He stood there wondering what that spot mean. Very soon, several doves come down—the blue and the white. The blue dove said to the young man, "This place is where we come together, we make big feast and dance. Then we go back to our home."

Doves all tame. More doves came, and the man sat on the edge of the beautiful place to watch them. Then two dove girls come by. One said, "Shoo." The boy looked up and reached out to catch one of the dove girls.

Then the girl say, "You must like me, that is why you catch me!"

"Yes." He replied. "I like you very well. You have nice red moccasins. I am going to take you on my journey."

"To where we go?" asked Dove Girl.

"Oh, just to the east to the pretty wide old world."

So, the two began on their journey for they are now married.

Dove Girl said to her husband, "I am going to tell you something very important. You must try hard not to break it. Please don't say to me, 'my wife.' If you call me that, you see me no more until you find a place called San Hilando."

Then they fix their bed and go to sleep. Next day, they continue traveling. They gather berries and sunflower seeds to eat. They travel this way for several days.

One night in his sleep, the young man starts to dream. He say, "My wife."

Right away, Dove Girl rose up and returns to San Hilando.

When morning came, the young man could not find his wife. He very sad now, and he know he had to find this place, San Hilando.

Toward evening, he comes to a mountain on the east where he finds the camp of the wind. The boy asks the Wind Boy for help. The Wind Boy ask, "What is it you want?"

"I must find a place called San Hilando. You have traveled on this flat wide world. Do you know of such a place?"

Wind Boy sat still and thought. He study and scratch his head but did not know of such a place.

"I am pretty young. Maybe my father might know of what you speak."

Father Wind reply, "I have been far and wide, even in some deep caves, on the flat wide lake. Also high above. No, I have never heard of that place but I will go and ask my old father. He is an old, old man, hard of hearing and his eyes are very dim. All he does is sleep. But I will try to wake him. He does not feel much and the only way to wake him up is to hit him with strong stick."

Old Father Wind is laying with his knees up, sleeping. The son hit him. He not move. He hit him again, and the old Father Wind raise himself and ask, "What you want?"

"Where is San Hilando?" both mens ask him.

Old Father Wind sat studying. "Lets see, San Hilando. I been over the flat wide world, flat wide lake, even in the dark deep cave and high above the thick fluffy clouds. But I never heard anyone mention that place. But there is one little place I have not been to yet so it might be the place you seek. I ask now that Young Wind Boy to go there. He is young, strong and fast."

Old Father Wind pointed to a high ridge and say, "Over that ridge is the place I never visited. It is over and down a little draw and you come out at the edge by heavy timber. It is open, pretty spot, sort of like small table."

Young Wind Boy went very fast to this spot. He saw a little house with a heavy, large woman in front shaking a rug. Wind Boy blew past the large woman so fast she drop the rug, and her skirt fly up, and she cry, "EE Yah! Here is place called San Hilando."

When Young Wind Boy returned to his camp, Father Wind asked what he had discovered.

After Young Wind Boy told what he found, Father Wind said to the young man looking for his wife, "You go follow his track."

Before the young man left the wind camp, he gave some tobacco to Old Father Wind for his trouble.

Just before the young man arrived at the small house, he stopped at the edge of heavy timber and put on the gray hat so nobody can see him. On the west side of the small house, he saw a smaller one. It is the home for the doves. It is late now, and the doves begin to return to their home for the night. Finally, the one he was looking for, the Dove Girl with the pretty red moccasins, flies in.

The young fellow comes over and says, "I come after you, so now we go!"

Thus the two escape from San Hilando. The sun is rising high, and they come to bank of small lake.

"Now it is time to hide," say husband. Dove Girl lies down by the side of the lake, and she turned into the bank. Her husband jumped to the middle of the water and changed himself into the cattail reed.

Now, the large old woman went to feed her doves and right away she knew one of her favorites was missing. The other doves told her what happen. She go out and catch her horse and start after the man who stole her pretty dove.

Pretty soon, it is time to hide again. This time both change to lay down beside the lake, Dove Girl on the east side and her husband on the west. They both turn into lake banks.

The old large woman come again searching all around. She saw no sign but knew they must be there. She thought and thought. If she drank all the water up, then the two would have to come out from somewhere. So, she started to drink.

She drank and drank. She drank a whole lot of water—too much. She burst, and there she died!

The two rose up and traveled very fast to the camp of the husband. There they live very happy, with plenty of wild fruit for them, and all kinds of game.

This happen many years ago.

How Old Brown Turkey Got His White Tail Feather Markings (A Tale of the Great Flood)

One of Percy's favorites and told in one form or another by others, the tale of how the brown turkey got his white wing markings is amusing and whimsical. Many of the elders remembered that story, and it was at one time, when Percy was a boy in the late 1890s–1900s, a tale that every Apache child knew. It also brings to mind a simplified version of the "great flood" narratives common to most tribes and cultures worldwide. Eve Ball related this version on many occasions much as Percy and others repeated it to her.

Ussen warned the Apaches that there was to be a time when they would have days and nights of rain and that they must prepare for it. That was a long, long time ago. It was before the time of the Great Vision, when the Apaches still had hope. They were to gather all kinds of food, both for people and for animals. They were to take a male and female of each kind of bird, beast and even things that lived under water.

They were to go to the top of the mesa overlooking the Great Canyon, and there they were to use juniper and cedar to make frames for shelters. These were to be covered with the tanned hides of animals. That would provide shelter for all the people and their supplies. Some Apaches believe that all this happened at the same time that the man in your sacred book [the Bible] got his orders.

Then the Apaches were told to go again to the top of the mesa and dig long ditches leading to the canyon so that the water might drain into it.

It was to be eight hunting seasons before the big rains came, so there was plenty of time. No one was to rest until the stores had been gathered and prepared for use. Each man, woman and child was to do his part and to do it well. It was a long distance from one place to another where food could be harvested in season, and this was before the Apache had horses and they had to carry most things on their backs. A few had trained dogs to help with loads, but most used the burden basket. And though they worked hard and long, their religious observances were never neglected. Each brush arbor or teepee faced the east, and at the first sign of dawn, the men stood in the entrance with faces and arms raised to pray to *Ussen*.

Soon, everything was ready. Apaches do not like to hurry, but if it is necessary, they can. When the rains first came, it was only a slow drizzle, but it brought the animals to the top of the mesa, and that was long before the water began rising.

One of the very last pairs to start the ascent was old brown turkey. Both a male and female were seen, but strangely, neither appeared until after all the others had arrived.

The Apaches watched at the edge of the canyon's rim every day, wondering what had become of the turkeys. Finally, a few warriors decided to go down there looking for them. The rain was now coming down so fast that they could barely see, and the water began rising until they thought they would have to swim. Then one warrior saw the hen turkey trying hard to climb the hill before the water overtook her. As turkeys do, the foolish thing stopped at times to look back, instead of trying to reach safety. The man picked her up and took her to the mesa top.

Another warrior saw the male turkey, water-logged, slowly dragging his body upward. He motioned for the other Apaches to come and watch the gobbler making his desperate effort to escape the flood. As they watched, he finally made the top and fell from exhaustion. But he still was not safe in one of the prepared shelters.

The rain was coming down now in torrents and churning up a frothy white foam. In fury, it lapped at the mesa's edge. The gobbler was too tired to move any higher.

Young Apache warriors with turkey feathers in their war caps. *Photo by Eugene Heathman, editor of the* Ruidoso Free Press.

The warriors had had no merriment for some time, and because they could not condone weakness in themselves or their people, they talked to the turkey, saying, "You are lazy! Come up higher or you will drown."

But the gobbler could lift only his head and that in despair. His wings were lying back toward his wet, bedraggled tail, and he could hardly move. The oil was gone from his water-soaked feathers, and they were too heavy for him to lift.

The foam lapped over his tail and the tips of his wings, leaving rows of white. Finally, one Apache came to the water's edge and lifted the almost drowned turkey and placed him under a shelter. In time, the foam dried, and the brown turkey of Mexico and the New Mexico highlands to this day has marks on his tail and wing tips from the white foam of the Great Flood. Turkey feathers are used for war decoration on caps and shields to this day.

Chapter 10

LEGENDS OF CAVES AND BATS

The frame of the cave leads to the frame of man.
—Stephen Gardiner

A bat is beautifully soft and silky; I do not know any creature that is pleasanter to the touch or is more grateful for caressing, if offered in the right spirit. I know all about these coleoptera, *because our great cave, three miles below Hannibal, was multitudinously stocked with them, and often I brought them home to amuse my mother.*
—Mark Twain

For as the eyes of bats are to the blaze of day, so is the reason in our soul to the things which are by nature most evident of all.
—Aristotle

Because of the Apache reticence to talk about certain secret rites, I have presented only general comments with regard to the role of caves and their significance to the Apaches. Their views are merged below with examples and events. I am indeed grateful for the assistance of these individuals, whose ages range from middle age up to late seventies. Eve also recorded instances of cave legends or information about bats and the nether world, but in general, it is a topic little discussed with others not of their culture.

Apaches were very observant of the world around them, as we have learned. They also noticed the flying creatures that were not birds, yet unlike any other animal in their environment. On occasion, they were considered in folktales as tricksters, much like coyote but not as clever or popular. While Apaches did not draw or paint bats, there are a few intriguing folk tales about caves and bat people. Percy and his father also told stories about bats. These tales include lands as far southeast as the famous Carlsbad Caverns/ Guadalupe Mountains, as far southwest as the Tres Hermanas near Deming and north up to the Sacred Mountain, Sierra Blanca. Near Sierra Blanca, Fort Stanton Cave is another location that enticed both early settlers and, before them, the Apaches. Bats inhabit all of these caves.

Throughout history, mankind has made use of caves for shelter, burial or as sacred sites. Caves are considered to be places of *Power* and *Danger*, and to some tribes they are sources of their origins. The Aztecs of Mexico claim in their myths that they came from a land of *seven caves* far to the north. Each group left their caves and migrated south, establishing major cities within the interior of Mexico before the Spanish conquered them in 1519. Scholars to this day cannot agree where Aztlan is although some believe it to be in the Southwestern United States. Others give a date of AD 1064 when Sunset Crater in Arizona exploded, spewing forth death, destruction and fear among native peoples. Among these were the tribes from the seven caves, and hence we also have mysterious legends about Aztec gold hidden in many caves throughout Apachería.

We have also learned about the four sacred mountains of the Apaches and recognize that there are significant caves located in each area. Almost every one of these caves involves a legend or reports about people who can go to the entrance and hear songs, music or words coming from beneath the earth. However, not all individuals can hear these things. If one is serious, then a song or some kind of *Power* will come to a medicine man or woman or individual who needs the blessing of the gods. The concept of *Power* is an innate part of the Apache culture and is sometimes difficult for the non-Indian to comprehend. How you used that *Power* was up to you. It was utilized for good or evil. Old Nana's *Power* was two-fold. He had the *Power* over rattlesnakes and also the ability to find ammunition for his warriors. Geronimo believed he was impervious to bullets. Lozen had the *Power* to locate the enemy and was a valuable member of Victorio's warriors as they fought the U.S. Cavalry.

Caves are the entrance to the underworld, and therein is the *Danger* factor, fear of the unknown. Both good and bad medicine can come from caves. One recent example can be found when Highway 70 through Mescalero was being widened. Many of the Mescaleros were against it because they feared this construction would destroy a very important but small cave and potentially release "bad medicine."

Mescalero ceremonial grounds, circa 1920. Inside teepees, preparations of dancers are being made as they would have in caves during the long ago past.

The Crown Dancers (*Ga hé* or Mountain Spirit Dancers) have a repertoire of stories about caves and preparing for ceremonies inside caves, especially in the old days. Today, most of these preparations are accomplished inside a teepee or brush arbor.

Bats have played an important part in folklore on a worldwide scale: in China, the Pacific Island nations and the land of the Maya in Mexico and with numerous other North and South American indigenous groups. European stories about bats exist, of course, but they are usually gruesome and involve bats in a terrible and frightening light.

Mostly bats just want to be left alone to eat tons of insects. Numerous plants within their realm in the Southwest and Mexico are night blooming, and therefore insects and bats prefer to feed in the nighttime hours, hovering over these blossoms without anyone observing them. There is an important reliance, however, one upon the other, and some of these plants provided food for the Apaches. The yucca, *datil*, *sotol* and others would be among those pollinated by bats.

Knowing the land the way we do today, it is sometimes difficult for us to imagine the feelings of an early Apache or member of the ancient Desert Culture as they first viewed the entrance to such a large cave like Carlsbad or even Fort Stanton Cave. "Overwhelming" might be a good description, as they no doubt observed the millions of bats coming out of the mouth of these caves.

The indigenous people may have gone a short distance inside Carlsbad, but the steep drop-off could have kept them from exploring much beyond that main opening. There are pictographs at the entrance and many mescal roasting pits on the nearby hills.

Fragments of sandals have been found inside the cave, and parts of ancient torches have been found inside Fort Stanton Cave. Of course, nearby Feather Cave and Arrow Grotto along the Bonito River were considered sacred ground for many of the Jornada Mogollon peoples. No doubt the Apaches were aware of each of these caves.

There are also numerous stories about soldiers chasing Apaches into Fort Stanton Cave and then camping at the mouth of the cave while waiting for the Apaches to escape. However, the report was that the Apache never came out, yet later it was noted that their horses had been recovered and gone from the very place the Apaches left them. Was there another opening? Did they really escape? No one can answer those questions.

It was not until the Anglo ranchers and settlers came into the area that the Guadalupes and Carlsbad were explored by curious individuals like cowboy Jim White, who discovered the Carlsbad cave in 1901. He claimed he worked his way through the rocks and brush until he found himself gazing into the biggest and blackest hole he had ever seen, out of which the bats seemed literally to boil. He couldn't estimate the number, but he knew that it must run into millions.

The next series of legends is about caves in sacred places and stories about dancers, bats and those who lived beneath the earth. They will be unlike any you have ever heard. The first one comes to us from interviews that Eve Ball had with the Jones Boys (from Carlsbad and Seven Rivers) and Percy Bigmouth.

The Flight of the "Evil" Ones (as told to Eve Ball)

Ironically, a wonderful account obtained about Old Scout Bigmouth as a younger man and the entrance to Carlsbad Caverns comes through the many interviews with the Jones family, who had settled in the area. Ma'am (Barbara) Jones, the mistress of the house and a strong woman of the frontier, was respected by just about everyone. Her strong and rambunctious sons played or hunted with the Mescalero Apaches, and her husband had befriended several. The Apaches were often hungry and tried to get passes to hunt in the nearby Guadalupe Mountains. It just wasn't fitting somehow, Barbara Jones thought, that they had to obtain passes to hunt on their own lands.

This time, her son, Jim, was to go along with them on a special hunt. The Apaches had taken good care of the boy on shorter stays and delighted in trying to teach him their ways.

Old Magoosh, the Lipan, was one allowed to go, and so was Bigmouth. The "pass" was for two weeks and for twenty men. No doubt women would also go along to cut the meat and jerk it. Barbara Jones baked bread and sent a good supply of other food too. Her son loaded it onto a packhorse. Meeting up with the Apaches at noon, they all ate handfuls of jerked venison and ground mesquite beans, but they did not stop to eat. That was the way they often traveled, eating on the move. They continued the trip until, at sunset, the warriors killed two deer by a small stream. Continuing on, they ended up at a place now called Rattlesnake Springs. A lush, riparian area with cottonwoods and a virtual paradise in the desert country, it was a favorite camping place for the Apaches.

Bigmouth explained to Jim that on a nearby ridge, there was a huge opening in the earth. It was a deep, dark hole and was a forbidden place. It was referred to as the home of the Evil Ones. Later, of course, this was to be known as Carlsbad Caverns. Naturally, the boy wanted to see this gaping, mysterious opening.

Later, in the 1960s, Eve Ball interviewed the entire surviving Jones family. It is interesting to have that family describing how Bigmouth and the Apaches viewed the cave.

Jim wanted to know who or what were the Evil Ones. Bigmouth was vague in his response, other than to state that it was a dark hole and those who entered never returned. Only the flying ones came out. He called it a death hole.

When Jim kept pressing for information as to what these "Evil Ones" looked like, Bigmouth stated, "Like smoke, filled with countless tiny things, specks like birds. I have seen one; it was the 'scout' who came first from the cave to look about and give the signal for the rest. Soon it will come from the earth and fly upward in circles looking all round. If the scout thinks it good, the evil ones will follow, many as the leaves of grass, and the scout will lead them upward like smoke. And they will go to the far away. I have seen this."

Naturally, Jim had to view this phenomenon that so frightened his friends.

Bigmouth agreed but claimed they must wait and be hidden from sight. Settling in until dark was difficult at best for the impatient boy. They hid within a large mescal pit on the mesa and waited. The sun sank behind the purple-hued mountains. The Guadalupes turned flaming red and were surrounded by burnt orange wispy clouds.

Then Bigmouth gestured with his mouth over toward the opening. The scout came flying above. It flew higher and higher, and then it was followed by others, separately at first and then in groups, until a smoke-like spiral rose above the mesa and disappeared in the distance. It was, of course, the now world-famous flight of bats.

Jim, like all people who have ever seen this flight, was in awe. He asked Bigmouth if it happened every night. He was assured that it happened like that every time Bigmouth had been in the area and had for many years.

Jim wanted to explore into the depths of that huge hole. Bigmouth said no, telling him that it is "*muy malo*, very bad and evil," and warning him, "If you go, you won't come back."

So, for at least that trip, Jim was not allowed to go into the cave. Years later, of course, most of the family had visited the cave, but the first flight of bats was an amazing adventure for the young boy.

That particular summer night, he also asked his friend to tell more stories, but Bigmouth said no, saying, "Summer is not the time to tell story. You come to us in the winter when the snow comes. Then our people sit about the fires in the teepees and our old men tell the stories. Come to us in cold weather and you may listen to their talk and learn."

And so he did for many years to come.

How Soldiers Disappear into the Secret Mountain (As Told to Eve Ball)

The Apaches, like many indigenous people, had caches of supplies hidden carefully throughout their home country or en route to various places for hunting or defense. Deming was a crossroads for such activity. This area is fitting because one of the four sacred mountains is within that region. Originally, it had been considered a sacred place to the Chiricahua. However, once they were released from their twenty-seven years as prisoners of war and came to Mescalero, this union caused the Three Sisters area to become

Las Tres Hermanas. *Photo by Jon Stephanoff. Courtesy Kristine VanPool.*

special to the Mescalero as well. Thus over time, many of the attributes and legends of both bands are so intermixed that it is sometimes difficult to separate them from one another.

The Three Sisters (*Las Tres Hermanas*) is a place where visions can be seen, medicinal plants found and songs of the Mountain Spirits can be heard but only by properly prepared or purified individuals. There is a story about an elderly Apache woman being driven through Deming on her way to Arizona. Suddenly, she exclaimed and gestured with her mouth in the time-honored way of pointing by Apaches and Hispanics alike. It meant, "in that direction." She was excitedly explaining that there was a cave, *más allá* (over there), somewhere in those Three Sisters mountains. She said, "Long ago, some of us found mescal, meat and cloth. We were starving. Our dresses were torn, and we had no shoes. It was a bad time for us but we found that cave and it saved us!"

There could well be other caves or overhangs (even today) that are hidden behind trees or boulders throughout Apachería. Cowboys would find them once in a while, although not so much anymore. Sometimes the military located caches and destroyed them by burning every bow, every bolt of cloth, everything. One cave in particular had gunnysacks, bridles, saddle blankets, lace, hatchets, bolts of colorful calico cloth and general supplies. It was an amazing find. Covered with *sotol*, local grass or hay, and then topped with over a foot of dirt, the supplies were well hidden. People surmised that Victorio's men could have buried the items after one of their infamous raids from thirty or forty years earlier. Or they could have been concealed by Apaches coming across the line from Mexico to visit relatives in Arizona and New Mexico during and up to the 1930s. Old habits of survival are difficult to break.

Percy and others told Eve Ball the following soldier story that included this same area.

It is said there used to be a mountain south of where Deming is, and Apaches went there to dance. It is a sacred mountain. In it there is a canyon and a spring. One time they were all around that mountain. One woman and her son went out on the flat land to gather some seeds for food but went too far from the foot of that sacred mountain. They got lost.

They out there and cannot see far. And before they know, soldiers circle all around them. This is not good.

"Look, Mother! There Blue Coats!"

The soldiers saw the two Apache. In those years, they always travel with scouts. The scout called. "You know how far you going to go? You watch that sun and you will see."

In those later days, the scouts were considered traitors to their people for tracking them down to the depths of their secret camp sites, and the woman shouted back, "You shut up. You do what I tell you. You come over here and we going to cut your neck!"

She brave woman.

The bugle blow, and the soldiers come close. She been going backward toward the mountain, and she speak to the Secret Mountain. "Today, with you looking at me, I don't want nobody to do bad things to me."

Soldiers came with swords ready. She call again to the mountain, her brother. She turn to it and made the Apache distress signal. Nobody can refuse to respond to that sign. Nobody can tell you how it is made, as it is just for Apaches. She turn around. Soldiers riding their horses right into that mountain. You can't see nothing after while but their boots, and the horse's feet sticking out. And lots of saddles laying around. For many, many years, you could see those things. Maybe if you go there now, some of them are still left.

People watch from the mountain, and they couldn't understand what became of soldiers until she told them later around campfire. And that is how Sacred Mountain save that woman and her son.

The Cave of White Rocks (As Told to Eve Ball by Percy Bigmouth)

This old lady was out picking some juniper berries for medicine. Her daughter and son was around with her too. She see big bear. She tell the childs to climb a tree. And she stand with her knife to face bear. It too strong. It kill and eat her. Then it take off. The childs crying for their mother, and they don't look where they are going. They come up against a hill some place, and lots of white rocks.

A clown in white (breech clout) come up to them before they see him and asks, "Well, what you crying about?" The boy tell him bear eat mother. The clown say, "I take care of you. I carry the little one and you give me hand." They travel toward a big wall; and there is a little trail up the side, very steep, very narrow.

The childs afraid, "Oh, we fall!"

"Don't be afraid; you not fall," Clown said.

They go over that trail to the main place. Clown have a little stick, and he open the door in mountain. They see all kinds of animals in that cave like mean mountain lions, bear and wolves. They see skunks and rabbits. They see bats. They see rocks and they white and shiny.

"Come with me and don't be afraid; you not be hurt." They go four places, dangerous places. In the last one, they see Chief, old, white haired.

"Why you come?" ask Chief.

"Tell him," said Clown.

They did.

"You children of earth. In this cave, in this place you will starve."

Clown say, "Ask him for long, good life."

Chief say okay. "Now, go over there." Old Chief sits by his wife. Clown tells him again what happens.

"No people from outside allowed here," say Chief to them.

"We lost our mother; we hungry."

"The bear that killed your mother is dead now. See over there." The childs saw the bear with a chain around neck. "That the one that kill your mother. Now, I give you food and send you back to your own people. Clown will take you." When the Clown left them he gave each one an ear of corn. It satisfy their hunger. They don't know why. Then Clown say, "Over there are your people. I watch till you join them."

And, when the son and daughter find their people, Clown turn back, disappears into the cave.

After they got older, the boy and his sister return to the mountain. They find the bluff or wall and the narrow trail. But the opening into the cave was covered with chunks of rock. Among them was some, white, and soft. Chunks of it stuck out of the side of the canyon. They had learned what it was by this time. It was silver. But the Apaches did not want silver—too soft for bullets.

It was stated that many years later, some other Apaches went with them, and they camped and stayed three days and nights looking for that silver but never found it.

Son of the Rainstorm Hidden in a Cave

Even Geronimo, whose power was immeasurable throughout Apache history and legend, spoke about caves. His tales will be included because Geronimo influenced all Apaches, no matter their band affiliation, and many of his relatives live at Mescalero today. Several were known to Percy and his family. One account is of the legend of creation, and the other is a battlefield scenario.

*A caring mother dug her own cave and hid her child from the dragon. While this story is not of Mescalero origin, the people at Mescalero appreciate the lore behind that section in his autobiography (*Geronimo, His Own Story*) relating to the creation of the Apache. The term "dragon" is probably a mistranslation because the man helping with Geronimo's autobiography was of Anglo tradition, and a dragon was as horrible as Big Owl or any monster. The story is essentially the same as we have seen in the tale in which White Painted Woman bears Child of the Waters. The names are different, but the lessons and origins are the same. All Apaches love the story about how the child and his mother outwitted the monster.*

Geronimo, feared leader and guerrilla fighter, told his story to E.M. Barrett, describing cultural events of the Apache way of life. He was, according to General Nelson A. Miles, "one of the most resolute, determined-looking men that I have ever encountered."

Among the few human beings that were yet alive was a woman who had been blessed with many children, but these had always been destroyed by the beasts. If by any means she succeeded in eluding the others, *the dragon*, who was very wise and very evil, would come himself and eat her babes.

After many years a *son of the rainstorm* was born to her and she dug for him a deep cave. The entrance to this cave she closed and over the spot built a camp fire. This concealed the baby's hiding place and kept him warm. Every day she would remove the fire and descend into the cave, where the child's bed was, to nurse him; then she would return and rebuild the camp fire.

Frequently the *dragon* would come and question her, but she would say, "I have no more children; you have eaten all of them."

When the child was larger he would not always stay in the cave, for he sometimes wanted to run and play. Once the *dragon* saw his tracks. Now this perplexed and enraged the old *dragon*, for he could not find the hiding place of the boy; but he said that he would destroy the mother if she did not reveal the child's hiding place. The poor mother was very much troubled; she could not give up her child, but she knew the power and cunning of the *dragon*, therefore she lived in constant fear.

Soon after this the boy said that he wished to go hunting. The mother would not give her consent. She told him of the *dragon*, the wolves, and the serpents; but he said, "Tomorrow I go…"

This story, as most legends do, meanders back and forth weaving a tale of cunning and frustration but of course ends well for the Apache people, as we have seen in Percy's similar version.[15]

Battlefield Visions (Entering of Ussen's Land [Heaven] from a Cave)

Geronimo also spoke of a cave and a warrior while lying unconscious on the battlefield. The visions he encountered begin with a simple mulberry tree growing out from a cave and had been repeated by many older warriors.

Before this cave a guard was stationed, but when he approached without fear the guard let him pass. He descended into the cave, and a little way back the path widened and terminated in a perpendicular rock many hundreds of feet wide and equal in height. There was not much light, but by peering directly beneath him he discovered a pile of sand reaching from the depths below to within twenty feet of the top of the rock where he stood. Holding to a bush, he jumped off from the edge of the rock and dropped onto the sand, sliding rapidly down its steep side into the darkness. He landed in a narrow passage running due westward through a cañon which gradually grew lighter and lighter until he could see as well as if it had been daylight; but there was no sun. Finally he came to a section of this passage that was wider for a short distance, and then closing abruptly continued in a narrow path; just where this section narrowed two huge serpents were coiled, and rearing their heads, hissed at him as he approached, but he showed no fear, and as soon as he came close to them they withdrew quietly and let him pass. At the next place, where the passage opened into a wider section, were two grizzly bears prepared to attack him, but when he approached and spoke to them they stood aside and he passed unharmed. He continued to follow the narrow passage, and the third time it widened and two mountain lions crouched in the way, he had approached them without fear and had spoken to them and they also withdrew. He again entered the narrow passage. For some time he followed this, emerging into a fourth section beyond which he could see nothing: the further walls of this section were clashing together at regular intervals with tremendous sounds, but when he approached them they stood apart until he had passed. After this he seemed to be in a forest, and following the natural draws, which led westward, soon came into a green valley where there were many Indians camped and plenty of game. He said that he saw and recognized many whom he had known in this life, and that he was sorry when he was brought back to consciousness."[16]

Eve Ball verified the description of the Apache idea of heaven. Both Daklugie and Percy told her she would like the Apache Heaven: green forests with game and plenty of water and beautiful land. She agreed and said it sounded perfect, but she liked books and libraries, which she doubted would be in their heaven. Daklugie laughed and told her, "Ms. Ball, we Apaches will make a raid on your White Man's heaven and that Library. We will bring you as many books as you wish."

Well, how could she argue with that?

The Dance of the Mountain Gods

There is nothing more striking and exciting than to sit around one of the roaring fires during the famed Mescalero Fourth of July ceremonies and see the War Dance that has changed little since the pre-1880s time frame and the Dance of the Mountain Gods that represents the very essence of the Apache worldview. One thing to always remember, according to Percy and many others, is that one must always look into the fire.

Percy would take "Old Dad" with him when he was feeling good, even up to the time when he was very elderly. It was just part of that tradition, and it was a source of renewal for the aged Apache and for his sons and their families.

Crown Dancer
during Fourth of
July ceremonials.
*Photo by Erik
LeDuc.*

The drum throbs as singers begin the ancient chants. There is nothing like hearing that sound. Then five dancers appear. Four have the upper bodies painted black with different symbols of a particular group painted in white on the chests and backs. They are known as Ga hé. A carved headpiece is decorated and tied over the mask. There are leggings and moccasins of buckskin, and dancers carry a traditional broad wooden sword in each hand. The fifth dancer is also masked and painted in white and is referred to as "clown." They all stomp, sway, posture and prance. The flames of the fire cast shadows and light on the feast grounds. The people watch in awe. The children are quiet. The dancers are in control.

Apache Crown Dancers or Ga hé are feared and respected by all.

Most visitors today who are non-Apache only see this aspect. Most of them do not know the history of this revered dance and how the old Apache legend of the first men who saw these mountain spirits reflected goodness and salvation.

This following version is a combination of the Chiricahua/Mescalero tale and Percy's story as translated from his father, "Old Dad." Each band embellishes, adds and deletes from the story depending on the storyteller.

Long time ago, two young men, one crippled and the other blind, were left in an isolated mountain cave. This was so because their band had been attacked and they were fleeing for their lives. They did this so they would not slow the flight of the people. They also understood that as soon as their people could, they would be rescued.

Many days and nights they waited. What little food they had ran out, they became thin and they began to be afraid that they had been abandoned and that death would rob them of their life. Family would never again be seen.

Sitting huddled in the darkness, they began to hear strange and frightening sounds outside the cave. The sounds became louder, and the two were very much afraid. Then, into the cave came five dancing figures, four painted black with white symbols and the mythical head pieces and one painted all white with special clay paint. A light came into the cave, and the figures of the intruders stood out. Suddenly, a big fire came, and all around the fire, the men danced. They called up the wind and rain, and they fought unseen enemies with their swords made of mescal staves.

Both men hid in the very back of the cave, and they knew that the hunger must be making them see things, but still they believed these dancers had come for them.

These were strong gods who would help them see and walk again. At first they did not understand this, but soon the gods led them, the blind warrior and the crippled man, from the dank, dark cave. The white-painted figure struck a giant rock with his stave, and that rock divided to form a new passage.

Through the passage both men walked. And the blind man could see, and the crippled man could walk. Their rags turned into clothes of the best buckskin, and each held good bows and good arrows, beautifully made.

The Mountain Gods, as they are now known, disappeared, but the two men were no longer alone. They saw a *ranchería* in the distance. As they

Ga hé dancers. *Photo by Mary Serna.*

drew close, they saw it was the camp of their own band! Their people had survived. They joined them and told them about how they were healed. Then in honor of the Mountain Gods, these two men performed the dance, just as they had observed. Many generations later, the Apache have performed this Dance of the Mountain Gods to drive away evil thoughts and take sickness from the people and to bring good health.

At Mescalero when they perform these dances, the *"gahe-nde dance,"* most people no longer remember the story of the lonely men abandoned in that cave or the story of their survival. They view it as an interesting feature of the Fourth of July ceremony. But the Apache elders never forget how it all began. In the old days, they told these stories over and over. Today, though much has been forgotten in detail, parents still try to educate their children.

As Percy stated to Eve Ball, "So from generation to generation, the story of our people's way and the Mountain Spirit dancers symbolizes protection and our kinship with all of the land."

Woman Captured by a Bear (and Hidden in a Cave)

As the Lipans were changing their geographic regions because of warfare and encroachment, they seemed to get along with their Mexican neighbors—until Mexican cavalry tried to get them to act as scouts. Until that time, the two groups had lived in peace. Some shared this story of a Mexican woman and her bear captor. Evil spirits inhabiting the bear were always a part of the Apache belief system, and they would kill a bear only as they might a human being—in self-defense.

This version was incorporated into the Lipan/Mescalero conscience. Percy heard this from his mother's people and related it to Eve Ball during the years she interviewed tribal elders on the reservation.

So, here we go to Mexico where an old Mexican woman started up the mountain to gather healing herbs. She did not return to her village. Neighbors and family went to look for her. They search many days before finding her. Except for being tired and very scared she had suffered no harm. She told them that she had been captured by a bear! When it charged from a thicket she run very fast but was overtaken and caught by that bear. She expected to be killed, but instead the bear push and push and shove her up the mountain trail to a cave. The entrance was very low and the animal force her to wiggle through the cave on hands and knees. That very difficult and long way to go on hands and knees. Inside, it was very dark. She could see very little. The bear did not follow her but began pushing heavy stones against the opening. She could not escape. She fear that it might leave her there to starve. But that old bear left and then brought fruit of the *nopal* (prickly pear). The rich purple juice satisfied her thirst and the fruit itself was good for hunger. Part of her barricade had been removed when the animal give her food; and she thought that she might be able to push rocks and run. Carefully she wriggled through the passage only to find the bear on guard outside.

Each morning the bear checked the barricade before leaving the cave entrance and each evening it brought fresh food to her. After having been a prisoner for about a week, one morning after the bear leave she hear voices—voices speaking Spanish. They were her Mexican peoples. She crept as near the exit as she could and called loudly. The voices came closer and at each call she answered them.

She wait long time. Then a man she recognized came into her view. He ran to her with others following him, and they help her out of that cave.

It was almost sundown when they reached her pueblo. They saw that the bear was following them. He angry. In spite of their tabus, they killed the bear. Then these Lipans and Mexicans became friends. And, they also learned about Mescaleros living as a tribe in New Mexico. It would still take a while for them to return to that side of the border. However, for that time, they were all friends.

Bats—Mounted on Silent Silken Wings

...that nature made many a blundering trial with the scaled and feathered folk, but all her finished summing up of flight she centered in this her favorite, the high-born, cave-born Bat, that clad in exquisite furs, mounted on silent silken wings, equipped with wonderful senses, has so long led his blameless life so near our eyes, and yet so little on our ken.
—*Ernest Thompson Seton,* Wild Animal Ways *(1923)*

The following tales about bats are different from what we usually think of when bats are discussed. The reader will find them amusing and refreshing and a different, more intriguing view of what are generally considered to be blood-sucking creatures of the night.

Why Bat Has Short Legs

Long, long ago, Killer of Enemies promised to save the Apache people from the evil monster eagles. They roamed everywhere, flying here and there, and carried off little children.

One day, Killer of Enemies played a big trick on Monster Eagle and got him to carry him high into a nest on a big cliff. Killer of Enemies killed the eagles, all of them.

Big problem for Killer of Enemies. He did not know how to get down from the nest of Monster Eagle. Just then, he saw an old woman approaching. It was Old Woman Bat.

"Grandmother Bat," he called, "help me. Take me down from here."

Old Woman Bat looked all around, but she could not see anyone. She looked and looked. Killer of Enemies called out again and again. Finally, Old Woman Bat saw Killer of Enemies and began to climb and climb up to the nest.

"How did you get way up here?" she asked.

"Monster Eagle carried me up here. Help me down."

"Climb in my Burden Basket," she said. "I will carry you down." Killer of Enemies looked at the straps made of spider silk.

"Those straps are too weak. They won't hold me. They will break and I will fall," he said.

"Don't worry," she said. "I have carried Big Horn Sheep in this Burden Basket. Just close your eyes, and you won't fall. If you look, we will both fall."

Old Woman Bat began to sing a strange song as she began to climb down the cliff. Her Burden Basket swung from side to side. The wind moved it. Killer of Enemies was very scared. He opened his eyes to look.

That was bad for both of them. As soon as he opened his eyes, they both crashed to the bottom of the cliff. Old Woman Bat landed first and broke both legs. Killer of Enemies landed on her and lived. Old Woman Bat's legs finally healed, but they were short from that time on and that is why bats have short legs.[17]

Traditional burden basket. *Photo by James Sánchez.*

Why Bat Hangs Upside Down

Once, long ago, old Coyote really wanted a wife, but he did not know which woman to choose.

Bat said, "Why don't you take Hawk Chief's wife?" Hawk Chief had not been seen for many, many days. He had been missing for long time. Coyote thought and thought and decided it was good idea.

But Hawk Chief did return and became very angry. They say he was so mad at Bat for giving such bad advice to old Coyote that he picked up Bat and threw him hard into a juniper tree. Now, old juniper tree is a tough tree and strong. Bat was caught there with his long and pointed moccasins. He

The Mimbres (Mogollon) people included bats as part of their vast anthropomorphic art forms that were unique images on some of their beautifully designed ceramics. *Courtesy Pete Lindsley.*

was caught there upside down and could not escape. He twisted and turned and tried to get down.

And from that time on, bats have always hung upside down, even when they sleep.[18]

Part III

ON THE WAR TRAIL

Chapter 11

OF RAIDING AND WAR

From now on it will be war...war to the death. There is no other way.
—*Chihenne chief Victorio*

It is better to have less thunder in the mouth and more lightning in the hand.
—*Apache proverb*

All who have died are equal.
—*Comanche proverb*

Apache and Comanche were great horsemen and warriors. Both were beyond cruel in the way they captured and treated their enemies. Some would say the horror stories of torture are equally bloody and brutal for both tribes. Percy's written accounts do not include these details, but we know from other frontier diaries and reports that they were gruesome.

By reading Percy's accounts of conflict with the Comanches, one can garner a

Young Apache warrior prepared for war. *Photo by Eugene Heathman, editor of the* Ruidoso Free Press.

sense of history and cultural mores and obtain a basic idea of what life in peace and war was like for the people as they struggled with enemies and technological changes. Newer technology (rifles, cannons) or the capture and subsequent gentling of the horse, brought into their world by the Spaniard or Anglo, eventually became part of their culture, and the narratives changed accordingly.

Lipans Before Mescalero

As we have learned, before the Lipan moved into the Southwest, they had developed into a strong and handsome folk with a distinct culture and language. They had seen White Eyes and ships along the Gulf Coast. Perhaps these were Spaniards seeking new lands and empire for their king. However, once they settled at Mescalero they gradually merged with the dominant band, losing a good portion of their language and other cultural distinctions. One group has tried to reemerge in Texas with specific ties to Lipan culture.

Percy had a very good general concept of Lipan history and a more detailed one for the Mescalero since his father was Mescalero and very much involved in tribal/band affiliations. His mother, being Lipan, presented intriguing and colorful details as she wove her stories into their lives, although by the 1940s, Percy had adapted to the Mescalero way.

The Comanches were some of their most formidable enemies, yet on occasion they exchanged trade goods and, when they were not at war, often had good relations. However, as populations grew and leadership changed, the Lipan continued to be pushed farther west and south by the "Lords of the Plains."

The Lipan had once seen themselves as the major force in the regions where they lived, but the Comanche also viewed themselves as dominant. Conflict was a given. Both sides had valiant warriors, but eventually all Native American tribes succumbed to the fearsome power of the White Eye and the Spaniards' rifles and cannon. If these rivals had joined forces instead of having petty struggles among themselves, they would have been a devastating enemy, and we must never forget that.

During the 1930s and '40s, ethnographers found that little ethnographic material had been "published" about the Lipan. Today, that is no longer true. For decades prior to this, the Lipan Apache had basically been deleted from the records as the "reservation era" was beginning throughout the West. Texas and New Mexico were no different. There were enclaves of survivors—some in Mexico, and some in New Mexico—but for the most part, they remained hidden in plain sight, so to speak. As they assimilated into the dominant culture (Mexican or Mescalero), it became more difficult to separate out some of their folk tales. If it had not been for people like Percy Bigmouth, who straddled both worlds, Apache legends and folklore would only be from the point of view of the primary cultural group. Of course, much was shared in common, but there were enough differences to make the contrast enlightening and exciting.

Constant contact with the White Man created a problem when a serious epidemic of smallpox decimated the Lipan, and so wasted by warfare and disease, they were forced even farther westward. As we have learned, a few found a retreat in the southern spurs of the rugged New Mexico/Texas Guadalupe Mountains, where they encountered the *rancherías* or camps of the Mescalero Apache.

Another band of Lipan often crisscrossed the Rio Grande and settled in the neighborhood of Zaragoza, Coahuila. These southern Lipan, according to Lipan at Mescalero, became known as "Big Water People."

In 1870, when attempts were made to concentrate the Mescalero at Fort Stanton after the Bosque Redondo disaster, some Lipan were convinced to come in at that time. The year 1903 was another pivotal one as the handful of Lipan POWs who had survived a war of extermination waged against them in Coahuila were brought to Chihuahua City. Finally, when it became known that they had relatives on the Mescalero Reservation, efforts were made to successfully reunite them.

Both Chiricahua and Lipan struggled to find their way in an ever-changing world. Mescalero, New Mexico, had become the focal point for renewal, for gathering of lost or broken families and bands. The Chiricahua found a home there after their twenty-seven years as POWs ended in 1913. Much credit should be given to the Mescalero for their willingness to accept both groups onto their reservation. This generous gesture was not approved by all involved in reservation politics, however. Nevertheless, the outreach was made, and it has been a successful blending of bands into the Mescalero homeland.

Thus, Percy provides us with an important focus about the way things were not so long ago among the Lipan and Mescalero.

Before They Got Thick
(Relations with the White Eyes)

The following tale has been repeated in numerous books and/or accounts about the Apache or generalized versions of Native American folklore. First, it shows us the "Western/New Mexico" version of the Pilgrim legend, ie., Indians help White Man survive the elements and their own ignorance. The second reason is, of course, because it was related to several people by Percy Bigmouth. It was repeated to him by his mother, who had learned of it from her mother.

Also note that the vernacular of the Apache storyteller and the unusual punctuation we have observed in Percy's other stories have been eliminated by rather severe editing. However, the flavor of the tale still comes through as a valuable lesson in relationships between Indians and white men. It also provides further evidence of a Lipan/Apache connection to the ocean and lands far different than the ones they finally occupied in New Mexico. Both Percy and his father remembered the words about the Gulf Coast life of their ancestors, despite the fact that they never experienced it.

Through Percy's good memory, we have a colorful tale of cultural encounters with the White Eye.

My Grandmother used to tell this story; she told it to my mother. It is about the time when they lived near the Gulf. She says that they lived at a place called "Beside the Smooth Water." They used to camp there on the sand. Sometimes a big wave would come up and then they would pick up many seashells. Sometimes they used to find water turtles. They used to find fish too and gather them and eat them.

One time they had a big wave. It was very bad. They thought the ocean was going to come right up. It came up a long way. Living things from the water covered the bank, were washed up. Then, when the sun came out and it was hot all these things began to swell and smelled bad.

One day they looked over the big water. Then someone saw a little black dot over on the water. He came back and told that he had seen that strange thing. Others came out. They sat there and looked. It was getting larger. They waited. Pretty soon it came up. It was a boat. The boat came to the shore. The Indians went back to the big camp. All the Indians came over and watched. People were coming out. They looked at those people coming out. They saw that the people had blue eyes and were white. They thought these people might live in the water all the time.

They held a council that night. They were undecided whether they should let them live or kill them.

One leader said, "Well, they have a shape just like ours. The difference is that they have light skin and hair."

Another said, "Let's not kill them. They may be a help to us some day. Let's let them go and see what they'll do."

So the next day they watched them. "What shall we call them?" they asked. Some still wanted to kill while others said no. So they decided to let them alone.

The Lipan went away. After a year they said, "Let's go back and see them."

They did so. Only a few were left. Many had starved to death. Some said, "Let's kill them now; they are only a few." But others said, "No, let us be like brothers to them."

It was spring. The Lipan gave them some pumpkin seed and seed corn and told them how to use it. The people took it and after that they got along all right. They raised a little corn and some pumpkins. They started a new life. Later on the Lipan left for a while. When they returned, the white people were getting along very well. The Lipan gave them venison. They were getting along very well. After that, they began to get thick.[19]

Chapter 12

ENEMY PEOPLE (COMANCHES)

You see Gene, getting good Indian story and ledgen are hard to find it. I did this for you, cause you had been awful nice to me, Among the Indian the old ledgen, really meant a horse to them. That is they give a cigarrett and horse for them. Now these young geniration don't see it that way. They never try to learn them kind, too much of a white peoples way, Our young people done away with those stuff.
—Percy to Gene Neyland

As long as wind blows, his life and legacy will continue to twist and turn along courses only wild horses know.
—eulogy for Charles "Charlie" J. Chibitty, the last World War II Comanche code talker

From the time an Apache or Comanche boy could walk, he was prepared for war. It seemed like conflict was forever part of life, and so survival was always the key to training tactics. Both the Apaches and Comanches were horse people. Adults devoted much energy and attention to instructing their male children, but the girls also learned self-defense and how to wield knives and other weapons. Many tales of women surviving and fighting as heroines and not just as secondary figures are coming to the fore.

Among the Apache, Gouyen would be one of these inspiring female figures. Francesca, wife to Geronimo, and Lozen, sister of Victorio, would be others.

Eve Ball had been told many times that Apache children were rarely spanked or cuffed. They were instructed to bathe on the coldest day in the freezing waters of the Sacred Mountain to toughen the body. They were directed to run, sometimes to the top of a mountain or over wide desert lands. The young Apaches did this because they had been ordered to do so. It was imperative among all members, especially the young warriors, to be disciplined. It meant you lived.

The Apaches in general were especially adept at defending themselves, and some of their greatest tests were with the Comanches in battle. Percy's longhand written account is

"Percy in War Bonnet." Famous postcard image showing his Lipan/Plains heritage.

full of cultural references and is a treasure-trove for anthropologists and people wanting to know more details about these clashes. We now understand that Old Scout Bigmouth participated in that era of war and battlefield skirmish, and Percy has been our mirror into this life, as he both memorized and wrote out many of the accounts from his father and his father's contemporaries.

Percy was a skilled maker of weapons of war, including bows and arrows and, to a lesser extent, lances and shields. He also made war bonnets.

He described for Eve Ball how the Apaches made their bows and arrows:

> *Our local wood is used for bows. While oak is good at first it does not last long. It does not hold up in shooting. The best wood is wild mulberry that grow east of the Pajarito and in the malpais* [Carrizozo area volcanic badlands near the Mescalero reservation]. *It make a good bow that lasts. Locust is strong…We use the sinew of a cow or deer…The arrow also is wrapped with sinew. The long bow is spliced—lapped and pinned together and the splice covered with leather…The bow string would sting*

the wrist so we made bow guards of leather, used tough rawhide. Old-timers made a small groove to give it a straight go. The Lipan bow was about five feet high; our lances ten feet.

While the following folk tales and oral history accounts go along with the theme of war, paradoxically, the Comanche, Mescalero and Lipan all seemed to have what we might call a "love/hate" relationship. Sometimes they raided together or rode with Victorio into Mexico. Sometimes they stole horses and women from one another. Sometimes they banded together to fight the Mexican and the Spaniards, and sometimes the latecomers, the Anglos, were also victims of joint raids. In other words, there was a confused and dangerous maelstrom on the plains and deserts bordering the mountain havens that were preferred by the Mescaleros.

Because the following collection is long and more complicated than the previous tales, some explanations are incorporated into the narrative in parentheses. The reader should also note cultural and archaeological information within the stories that can be gleaned from Percy's words. For example, the information on marriage customs, slavery among the Indians, treatment of women and their conflicts with various enemies is intriguing. The blame game is interesting. For example, the Comanche captives point out to their own people that they were better treated as captives of the Lipan than Comanche captives. Also, note their manner of problem solving; geographic location descriptions; safety precautions when enemies attack and battle details; information on Madzil, a Comanche chief; and alliances. It is truly a treasure-trove of cultural data.

Lipan Apache and Comanche Fighting Story of Old Days

So here I'm writing the story of fighting between the Lipan Apache and Comanche; Comanches have been living on the northern part of Texas. Lipan Apache Country is on the southwestern part of Texas and across over Rio Grande on the Mexico side. The Lipan Apache goes back and forth across the Rio Grande to Mexico side. They are friendly with the Mexico people. As the story goes, Comanches always come and make a raid on Mexican people for horse's and the Lipan's get the blame for all the trouble. They even go up here around Mescalero Country and make a raid for the horses; although some of the Comanches are on good terms with the Lipan.

There are different branches of the Comanches, but what they want most is horses. They came to a Lipan Camp. The Lipan had some very good horses. Then they stole the horses away from the Lipan. One of the Lipan fellow gone after his horses, He track them.

One of the Lipan men said, the Comanches are always taken our horses, but we wait till that fellow come back. See what he had to say about the horses, Then the fellow came back and said, he can't find any of his horses, he said he saw the horse track all around, and all looked headed toward the east. The Comanches drove all our horses away, Then the Lipan started after them.

They follow the Comanche, and while the Comanche stopped and cook something to eat, a Comanche Chief was there and had his horse staked close by. A single Comanche girl was there too. Out on the raid with the Comanche, There was another horse which belonged to this woman. This woman was down at the stream while the men were eating. She saw the Lipan men and warned, Here come the Lipan; but she went back at an easy pace; She didn't run—she wasn't afraid. She thought the Comanche men were going to protect her and didn't hurry. She went to her horse and put her things on it, She went down to the stream to wash her feet. She had her things on, The girl got on her horse, the Chief mounted his horse too, They met the Lipan and had a real fight. Pretty soon the Comanche began to back off. When the woman saw her men weakening, She got off and took her things off her horse, She spooked the horse and let it go.

Capture of Comanche Woman

She began to walk toward the Comanche men, she was a big woman and couldn't walk very fast, The Comanche men passed her, When she fell behind, a Comanche fellow came back with a rifle, The Lipan men hung back a little, making believe that they were afraid. This happened twice.

The Comanche said to the girl, Run a little, When we both escape, we will go together: The Lipan man still followed. And came around the third time. He wanted to get that girl for himself: He thought he was going to save her. This time the Lipan leader said, all right, shoot that Comanche fellow, He will make more trouble; So the next time the Comanche came near, A Lipan man shot him, The Lipan continued to follow on after the Comanche mens.

One Lipan man went over to the girl then. And the Comanche stopped, turned, and shot at the Lipan man, They tried to make him go back, the Comanche sending many arrows at him, but he curled up behind his shield, all you could see of him was his ankles, They couldn't hit him, Then the Lipan fellow made up his mind, He charged and grabbed that woman by the arm and took a ride. The Comanche tried to shoot but didn't hit him, Now the Lipan were coming up behind and the Comanche had to run on or die.

So that Lipan man got the woman right there. He took a piece of cloth. He put it over a mesquite bush and made a little shade for her. She set there and she not try to escape, She had two pretty blankets in her bag.

The man went back and joined the fight again. You could see the arrows flying out from the Comanche side, They really had a fight. They fought fiercely, but can't do any better. Pretty soon three Comanche fellow began to sneak off through the mesquite brush. They thought the Lipan didn't see them. The Lipan man rode around in front of them on the horse he had taken from the girl. He came upon them, He recognized them. They were Comanche friends, who had stayed with the Lipan many years before.

Other Lipan were coming now. They were going to kill these three Comanche, who couldn't get away, but one of Lipan on horseback rode to the others, He headed them off, He said, Those three fellers are our friends. They used to be with us some years ago. We can't kill them, So they said to the three Comanche, in sign Language, you three go your way at once!

So these three went their way, Comanche said thank you, and they went as fast as they could. The Lipan fellow returned to join his party. They were still fighting. They carried on fighting, you could see the rest of Comanche rolling over falling, Comanche woman still waiting in the shade.

There came one Lipan, a poor slow fellow, He saw the woman was sitting there, The slow Lipan fellow saw the bag too, went and grabbed it, He took one of the blankets and gave one back to her, Then this slow Lipan fellow gone back to their camp while the fight still going on. Soon all the Comanche were killed, but the three who were allowed to escape.

The man who captured the woman also took the horse. Then the fight is over. They turned back to the Comanche woman, The man who had captured her took his blanket that he had used as a shade for her, He threw it over his shoulder and told her to get up and follow him, He told her to bring the bag, They went back to the horse the woman had been riding, He told her to get on and she did. The saddle, the bridle, everything was on the horse yet, This Lipan handed her bag and she put it on the saddle horn, They started. This man and woman were a little behind, It looked as if she might try to get away, but she never did. She just followed right behind them mens, At last they getting nearer to their camp, but they didn't go straight in, They had to stop a little way, and let the people at the camp know they were coming, So they made loud noise. They began to sing and rode on into camp,

They got off their horses, many Lipans were sitting around in a circle, Then they slapped their thigh. Some time they do that, when they had no pillow, They supposed to use the pillows, when they at their camp. Then some of the womens came and dance, Then all Lipan had their victory dance,

The Comanche woman was there, and she look in on all that. After the dance the man took the horse and the Comanche woman to his camp. Soon this Comanche woman could go anywhere she like to. One day someone wanted her to help them around at their camp. But her owner said, "No, You people have arm, you can do things for yourself."

The man who capture this woman did not marry her, He just took care of her. After she had been with them about three years one man, who had been captured years before, He Married her.

And that is the end of that story.[20]

Chapter 13

THE RETURN OF THE CAPTIVES

*But you, my own people, when you take captives, you make them slaves, you people
work them to death. But the Lipan treated me well, I went out after water myself;
They didn't tell me to do it. And in the same way I gathered wood, I learned how to
tan buckskin and scraped rawhide when I felt like it, I was well treated and was not
forced to work hard. They treated me like a member of their own family.*
—Comanche captive woman

*Note the manner in which Percy addresses the life experienced by captives and their treatment
among his people, the Lipan, in comparison to the Comanche. The back and forth of
continual raids must have been wearisome, yet that was part of life during those times. If
it was not the white men, it was a war party from a different tribe.*

Comanche Woman

Now to go back to the three Comanche men who were turned loose, this is
their story. They say, they got back to their own country and they said the
last time we saw our fighting men, they were having a tough time, They all
were about to be killed. But the young Comanche woman is captured and
safe, we think: They said the mens fought pretty hard, but still lose the fight.

When the news was heard among, them, the Comanche girl's father got
awful mad, So he took his pipe, put some tobacco in it, and walk over to the

chief, The Chief took a puff and so on among the others, They did the same too—puffed on the pipe, That the sign they plan return raiding on the Lipan Apache's. *[Note here the use of a pipe in war talk instead of "peace talk."]*

In meantime, the two captive Comanche are married now, They living with Lipan happily, They could go anywhere they wished to. But all these days, the girl's father busy getting the men, planning to fight the Lipan, and get his daughter back. So the girl's father went and took the lead, Down toward the south they rode, out to the Lipan's country. At last they came to a spring of water, They look around for the sign of Indians or horse track, Then they had reached the top of the little hill, further on down toward the south they saw some horses standing under the tree in the shade, So the leader send one of his men to look over the horses, He went and sure enough its an Indian pony, He got back to the party and said let's get ready to make a raid on them, So they started to round up the Lipan's horses.

But one Lipan fellow came around and saw what had been going on, He rode back then and told the Camp, The Comanche's are gathering up our horses, So the whole camp went stir up, The Lipan fellows getting their bow and arrow with their quiver and war shield. A few use their lance, They got their horses too, which they been staken nearby, Then they rode over the hill to look. Ever since they had a fight with them, when they captured the girl, the Lipans never had seen any Comanche.

Now they came to get the girl back from the Lipan, The Lipan had been expecting this trouble ever since they captured the Comanche girl. Then another Lipan fellow rode out toward the north, at the same day when the other Lipan saw the Comanche were gathering their horse's, This other came in and saw there a big camp way up further north, That where these Comanche came from, Then the Lipan began sending their womens and children further out to the south, so if the fight started, they won't be in the way, they be safe:

Then the owner of the girl and the boy, called them in, and ask them, If they like to go back to their own Comanche people: As their camp is up toward the north, If they wish to, They can go,

Then the young couple got their horse and rode out toward north. Just before they begin to fight, the two rode over the hill, and saw the Comanche mens, They rode to them. The two, told them! Our owner had send us back to you, our people. They told the Comanche mens that they had been treated very well, and they showed their things which the Lipan men gave them.

The boy said I have grown up among these Lipan. Many years ago I fell into their hand, but never had been treated rough, Then the girl's father said, I had been gathering the mens, to figure on to fight the Lipans. We just about to start out and Then you two came over the top of the hill.

But the girl's father still waiting for one more camp to come in, The girl hadn't see her father yet, as he was going out among the camp, when the girl got back, they send one fellow after the girl's father. He was so glad when the news reach him, Right away he turned back to his camp. There was his daughter with a young fellow, And this young fellow looked Lipan, Someone showed them where her folks live, they were there, got their belonging off their horses. She embraced her mother. When her father came in, she did the same, and cried for joy.

Her father had put up big teepee, The headmen all came in to hear, what their leader going to say; after his daughter got back from the Lipan, First they asked question of the woman, how she had been treated by the Lipan in all their days and years, She said the one who had captured me is a real man, He motioned for me to go into his camp. I went in and stayed with them a couple years. They never treated me roughly or made a slave of me.

But you, my own people, when you take captives, you make them slaves, you people work them to death. But the Lipan treated me well, I went out after water myself; They didn't tell me to do it. And in the same way I gathered wood, I learned how to tan buckskin and scraped rawhide when I felt like it, I was well treated and was not forced to work hard. They treated me like a member of their own family.

Gotsa

The Comanche still didn't believe it, They asked her questions for two days, They asked, who is that boy? She told them, he is a Comanche too. He had been captured many years ago, before I was captured, You must know, Some one must remember when the Lipan and Mexican captured six Comanche boys. The Mexicans gave them to the Lipan, He was so high. She motioned with her hand to show that he was about six or seven years old when he was captured. He grew up among the Lipan. He doesn't know his own language; he doesn't remember it well, Just few word, The other five Comanche boys are still among the Lipan. What I tell you is the truth,

But her people couldn't believe it yet. They didn't understand. The head chief was there. Her father was acting as a leader too. Then they called the boy, and she interpreted for them...We understand that you are not a

Lipan but one of our people. The boy said yes. I was camping out there with my people. Lipan and Mexican soldiers came, There was a big fight. Many Comanche children were captured. Five other boys and I were given to the Lipan. We played with the Lipan children, We were well treated. When I grew up I looked after the horses of the one who reared me, I watered his horses, But I wasn't forced to do it. I could go anywhere. I was not a slave, and the other boys were treated the same way;

Finally they asked the boy, You say you don't remember your own language. But do you remember what your people used to call you? He thought for a little while; then he said. Yes. That's the only thing I do remember. My father used to call me *Gotsa*. Then all the men asked among each other about the name, Finally one said, Yes, there's a camp far away which had a boy by that name.

They went to that camp and called the leader. He came over, and asked what the trouble. They said to him when he came in. Look at that fellow. Can you recognize him? He looked closely at the boy; he said nothing. Have you lost any boys or have your boys been captured? Yes, I did lost my son when he was a little boy. The Mexicans and the Lipan came to our camps and stole many children. My boy was among them, I called him *Gotsa*.

There he sits they all shouted! Then these two, father and son stood up, They embraced: The Chief of all the people asked; Well what shall we do? Shall we go on and fight with them or stop here? We must settle it, They all look at the girl's father! Then the girl's father said. I got the tobacco and held the pipe to your mouth. Chief, So that we would go down and fight the Lipan and find my daughter. That is the only reason I wanted to go. But now she has returned and brought back a boy who was captured and forgotten long ago. Now they are both back safely. So I don't care to go on with the fight, We stop here.

Their Enemy Came in Peace

Then the others said, Yes, that is right. Let us stay here. No use going down and fight and losing some more men. That would be neither fair nor wise: But now that they have treated our children well and given them their freedom, We change our minds.

The father of the girl said. I am going over to Lipan country and see, what kind of people those Lipan are: They have killed our men many times when we have gone to fight them. Its our own peoples fault. Now you talking about going to visit them in a friendly spirit. That's what we ought to have done at the first place.

Then the Comanche prepare to go to Lipan Country. They say, Let's take some present to give it to the family that took care of our children. They trade in Buffalo robe and Buckskin, in the trading store and They brought some Calico and Shawl and Blanket. After they got back to their camp, in a few days, they started out to the Lipan country. Next morning they came to Lipan camps, They were camping by a stream running to the southwest. The Lipan are not watching closely, Soon someone shout, Comanche's are coming, Everybody stir up the camp. Children begin to run out in the bush. The mens were ready, some Comanche rode over to the camp. In a sign language they say *no fight*.

For that day, their enemy came again but in peace. There were not many Lipan because most of them are camping in different places on the land.

But some more Comanche came, They figure on to make trouble, But the Fathers of the two say no trouble: We came to visit the family that took care of our children, Not to fight, as some of you mens figure on.

Then the Father of the girl took out the pipe and tobacco, They puffed, every one of them, Lipan man came, He too puffed the pipe, so did the rest of his party. Now some of these Lipan mens understood Comanche. There they held the Council, Friendly talk, since they all puffed on the peace pipe.

They were to have a big feast, in next day: The day came. They send the boy that understood Lipan language over to his friend that took care of him, The boy came in and the Lipan man said to the boy, son what is it you came over for. Then the boy told him, There will be a feast in that big teepee today, so they send me over to tell you, and you come with the rest of the mens, They all agreed to go over to the feast. A crowd of people was there, The Comanche were preparing a big meal, Soon all the things are ready, They ate together.

The Comanche took a pail of water to all who had eaten. They suppose to wash and wipe their hands, Then when the eats over, they called a council again. The Lipan head man was there and so too the Comanche,

We do not want trouble with you. We stay around our country, hunting the game. Buffalo, Antelope, and Deer, But all the time while we are camping here peaceably we like to look upon you people as a friend. But you never wanted it that way, We Lipan don't want to fight your people. But your men ask for it, That's how the fight start, then we kill your mens Also we lose some of our men too. If you want to be a friend as you say, We willing to stand by you, and help you against your enemies, And we need your help. When the enemies fight us. So now its up to you, I'm willing to do whatever you say. You are the chief,

Then the Comanche spoke. He said, We'll settle this now. He dug a little hole in the ground with his finger, a hole about four inches deep, He spat in it first, Then the Lipan chief spat there too. Then he covered it up. Then the Comanche said. We have both spat in there. We have buried our troubles. Then the Lipan Chief says it is just two of us, you and myself, Lipan says it for all my people. Like wise Comanche said the same. Now we must be like brother and sister after this time. We must have no more trouble. Then they all scattered and returned to their camps.

The girl's father had brought many presents. He thought of the man who had reared his girl. He went among the camps with the gifts. He finally found the man that he was looking for, The Comanche man said, here my brother. This is all for you, For your trouble in taken care of my daughter. When she fell into your hand, When you captured her, you treated her in the right way. Now you are my brother. Beside all the presents, he brought the man the finest horse he had in his bunch.

The next day the young man's father came over with his presents, He said to the Lipan man who had brought up his boy: My brother, I have gathered all these things for you. Ever since I heard about you, how you kept my son safe for me and treated him well. I have wanted to give you something. This horse and all these things are for you, I brought them a long way for you. The Lipan man was glad to have the horse and the other presents, He thanked the Comanche man. He said come tomorrow and bring your rope along. Come when we bring our horses to water. The Lipan man who had brought up the girl had said the same thing to the girl's father! The girl's father came the next day. He had his rope. The Lipan brought the horses in. There was one fine horse. The finest to be found, among his horses.

The Lipan spread a blanket out on the ground and told the Comanche to sit on it, Then the Lipan got his lance, He said, I give it to you, He took his finest buckskin clothes. These are for you. He said. He staked the horse near the camp, This too is for you, It sure fast out on a buffalo hunt, good horse to go out hunt on it.

Then the boy's father came to the other Lipan. The Lipan spread out a blanket and said to his Comanche friend, to sit down. He took the Comanche's rope and put it around his finest horse and led it back to his Comanche friend. He took his spear and his fine Arrow quiver of a mountain lion fur and also his buckskin clothes. I give you this fast running buffalo horse, and all these things. Since we became friend or brothers, Now you can go where you please, No more trouble between Comanche and Lipan. And that is the end of that fight story.

Chapter 14

THE BATTLE OF COYOTE MOUNTAIN

Victory and Bitter Defeat

As our enemies have found we can reason like men, so now let us show them we can fight like men also.
—Thomas Jefferson

The Lipan leader said here they come, So be brave fellows: We Lipan's had many fight with them before, But this will be a hard fight.
—Percy Bigmouth

For the first time in this account, we learn about another Comanche leader given the name of Madzil (Coyote). No other specific names are mentioned. Percy rarely gives the names of people because among the Apache, once a person has died, the name is not mentioned again. It is also significant because Percy describes an important alliance of Apache groups, including Chief Juh's Nednhi of northern Mexico, or Blue Mountain Apaches, as they are called here. Many people believed that Apaches did not depend on alliances. However, for the Lipans and others to be included here in Percy's own words and fighting in war as one entity is enlightening. There are also vivid descriptions of Apache and Comanche fighting strategies, significant because they are written by an Apache.

Here another story about the trouble with the Comanche, At this camp, there are Southern Lipan, the Northern Lipan, No Water Lipan: Then Mescalero Apache; Blue Mountain Apache from the North West of Chihuahua, Mexico. They all camping together, on the east side of the Rio Grande River, Where the Indian call a Mountain Coyote

Mescalero warrior painting by Mescalero artist Ignatius Palmer, circa 1955. *Photo by Pete Lindsley.*

Mountain. Madzil: Means Coyote Mountain. Today they call that mountain Davis Mountain.

Around that mountain, These Groups of Apache's had a big fight with the Comanches, It happened many years ago, When my old Dad wasn't born yet, (probably around 1850) Just couple year before he was born, I've heard, as the story been told to him, Then he told me this story. Today old Dad, Is ninety two year old, And today he's the oldest man among the Mescalero Apache, Here at the Mescalero Reservation living now, and he been in the old Scouts, when Victory (Chief Victorio) on the War path. Victory (Victorio) is a Warm Spring Apache Chief, His country is just west of the Hot Spring all that Country clear to Arizona line. Old Dad also been Scout again when old Geronimo was on war path, Victory had been wipe out, on the south side in old Mexico South of the city of El Paso, Victory was in the year 1875 to 1880. Then Geronimo trouble is 1880 to 1886. Old Dad had done a lot of good help to Uncle Sam when the Indian trouble going on in the country. I wish to say some more of his work [much of this has been included in the chapter on Scout Bigmouth], but we on the Comanche trouble with the Apache. So here we go again.

Chief Madzil

Apaches were camping around the Davis Mountain. Were nice rolling hills and plenty of all kinds of game there. The Apaches sure like that country down there. Also there are plenty of wild fruits, Which the Indians make a living on: They like Antelope and prairie-dogs, whole lot. Then one day came, The Comanche's had been out raiding down in old Mexico; There are large groups. Two high Chief were there with their mens, as they coming back, they cross the Rio Grande River and set out camp. They didn't know the Apaches were camping near too, Next day the Comanche started out for their own Country, Moving along and over the hill, They saw a bunch of horse's grazing around out in the flat, And one of the Comanche Chief said to his men's, there are some horses down yonder, Some of you men's must go out there, and drive them over to our bunch, Then the other Chief said No. It might be an Apache's horse's, If they are let them alone, But still the first Chief said; When I started out from my country, to raid, and take my weapons along with me, I don't look for to make friends with anybody:

But still the other Chief kept on asking to make a peace with the Apache's, He look around at his men's and said to the other Chief, Whose name was Madzil, Just look at these fine young men's. We didn't lose any of them today. Lets make a peace smoke with them, and have a merry time tonight, See all what bringing back home with, Lot of goods, and fine horses.

Chief Madzil still wanted to fight. The two chief had talk together and they came near had a fight among them self. They already had the Lipan horses round up together. Chief Mazdil said I fight them and take their wife and children back home with us, and make them work for us, The other chief said. Don't talk like that, These Lipan are hard fighter I told you. When they came up to the top of the hill, They saw few camps on their side, But the larger Lipan Camps were just over another small hill. The Comanche didn't see those.

While the two Chiefs argued, one of the Lipan men gone out to look for their horses, He saw them, and rush right back to the Camp, He's the only one been out that way, It was early in the morning,

The other Comanche chief keep telling Madzil to go over to Lipan camp, and give them little present. But Chief Madzil says, I mean it to fight with them. Chief Madzil said: Mens we are on the Lipan camping ground Get ready, fix up, Can't say what going to come out, Whether we come out alive or died here, In this bright day! The other chief got Mad too now. He said to Madzil, don't cry to me for help, cause you the one going to start this fight, I told you all in good way, But you don't listen to me, so we shall see before the sun goes down.

Madzil said I get their women's and children: In the mean time the Lipan spreading the news to the other's, They had their women's and children away from the Camp. The Comanches had their war paint on, Putting on their best clothes, They had the Lipan horses on one side.

The Apache's got ready too, they came together.

There are lot of them for so few camps, said one of the Comanche, They must have their main camp on the other side. The Apache came up, they looking down to the foot of the little hill. All their horses were rounded up. The Lipan Leader rode on the front of his men, they all in a line, You men's must be brave, Fight with them, that what they meant, by taken our horses, Fix up your bow and the lance, Today is our fight start, We didn't ask for fight. They the one's, so let's all charge together, you young men's be brave, you see, they think they are men's. So let's be men's too. We see who will be real men, before the sun goes down. Another Apache Chief spoke up, What that Lipan Chief says is right, We all men so we going to show those Comanche how we fight.

Once more the Comanche Chief said to his mens, I had tried hard to tell Chief Madzil to make peace with the Apache's, but he won't do it, So now let's fight with them the best we know how, I think we going to lose this fight, Cause I had fought with them before. But the trouble we had started, We got to fight. Then the Comanche came out in the open, The Apache came on too, The two Comanche chief on the front. Their Men's right behind them, The Lipan leader said here they come, So be brave fellows: We Lipan's had many fight with them before, But this will be a hard fight,

Then Comanche came charged on them, But the Apache stood their ground and fought, Drove the Comanche back, But their two chief keep on charging. The arrows flying all around, Some of the Apaches got wounded, only light flesh wound. They kept fight back and forth. The Apache's charged again push the Comanche's back. Then one of the Apache, the leader of Lipan jump off his horse, and started to use his lance, the Comanche turned around, and came after the Lipan, Couple of Comanche, fighting all around, Then this Lipan backing up, while two Comanche coming toward him.

There are lot of sharp Mescal (plants), While backing up, he had stumbling over one of the Mescal, and fell over. Right away the two Comanche ran over to him, and shot him with the arrow. Then another use his lance, stab him down, They killed the Lipan leader right there. Then the other Apaches got real mad, They charge them again, So the Apache lose one fellow.

The Comanche Chief Madzil said you Apache people are not men, Don't know how to fight, So just leave me alone, I go on with my stuff and the horse's which I took away from you people, You mens better go on back to your camp, and do women's work, Since you can't fight us, He put some nasty word in too. The Apache's said, let's get going. We had lost one good fighter, So they start out again, There are a lot of brother in law, father in law, When the Comanche use bad word, all the men's we finish them all. Back up in a line again,

And then another Lipan leader rode out on the front and began talking to his men's. While rode on talking, They heard a shot from Comanche side, At that time, this fellow had his pistol in his hand, the horse he rode is kinda jumpy, Then this fellow on a horseback fell off his horse. They look over him, been shot in his head, They all said. Hows that happen, from his own pistol, one of the shell been fired, but most of them believe Comanche had done it,

Then at the Apache camp, one of the old Shaman men been out hunting prairie dog, He's a great Shaman, he been out early in the morning, out west from their camp, When trouble is on the eastern side, He's one of the leading men too. After he came back from his hunting, someone came to his camp, and he just about to turn his horse loose, He didn't even notice the women's and children are leaving, Then he is told, there is a big fight going on, just over the hill toward the sun rise, So he tightening up his saddle, and rode over to see what the trouble. He came to his men's as he's one of their leaders too. They told him, the Comanche had got all their horses, and they said, they had already lost two of their Lipan chiefs,

Well he said. We fix them soon, He talked to the crowds, He said he make his Medicine, Then he rode back and forth four times, in front of the lines, Come back to the end, and stop there, Then he said, Alright go to them, be brave and fight them. They'll soon be going to turn their back, They all headed for the two Chief, When they coming toward with his men's, The shields moving around every which way, on both side, Then one of the

Apache leader spoke out, Stabbing the chief with the lance, the Lipans start to push the Comanche hard now,

You could see the Comanche men's beginning to fall off their horse's, On foot they had a real hard fight, Now they driving backward, The Comanche laying there and there; all over, They almost killed them all, They would if they keep on following them, Cause they use all their arrow, But the Apache taken the arrow which the Comanche shoot them with: and Then they killed one of the Comanche Chiefs.

Victory

The Comanche began to cry, after they lose their brave chief, who was the one that don't want to fight in the first place. Only Madzil still fighting, But soon they wound him too, but just a flesh wound, Then one of the Apache says let them go, So they all rushing for the pack horse's and mule, also the Comanche horse's, All those few Comanche left, had been wounded, They thought, they going to die on their way back, sure enough some did.

But Chief Madzil making his Medicine on the way, That help him get back to his own country. They said only seven of them left, they got to their own country half starving, Cause they can't hunt, been wounded, at last they reach to their camping, Made a signal with a smoke. They saw their signal smoke, and some of the Comanche men's rode over to them, Oh what a bad shape they were in, When they came to them, They began shedding their tears,

Then Chief Madzil spoke. When we started out from our country, we had been down to old Mexico, We had spent four month or little over, down there. Raiding the Mexican pack trains of mules and burros, We get lot of fine shawls and fine blanket also. Many bolts of Calico, and good many head of fine horses, We started back happy from there, Been in a fight with them Mexican soldiers, But we didn't lose any men down there, Coming back we had plenty to eat, as we got some heads of Cattles too, all coming well, We singing, as we coming back with them pack train Mules and Burros with them goods, Came back to the Rio Grande River.

The Indian, they call this River, *Reddish Water*, Alright says the Chief Madzil, We cross the *Reddish Water*, Without a trouble, on this side we made camp, We saw some horse track, and my partner said, There must be some Lipan Camps, cause we saw some horse track, Then Chief Madzil spoke! I like to say this, If we see them Lipan we fight them and take away their wife and Children, and bring them back. I Thought we wipe them out; But I had made a fool of myself, For Not taken other chief's word, when he said, lets go over in peace, and have a peace smoke. Its better that way, So we won't lose no men's, He sure right about saying. I thought I'm a good fighter, But that day, I've found it out for myself, Yes I did fight with some of them. But just running fight. When we drove their horses away from them, And I thought they are not much of a fighter, We done that several time before, thought that they were easy, But now, fought it out when stand fight—hand to hand, They're tough fighter, and he show them where he had been wounded, in the arm on the side, three places on the leg, also on the head, Good thing they didn't come around with their Spear, If they use that on me, I be gone. I look that way, I see my mens had staggering with the arrow on under their arm. I sure got scared, thought my end is coming, Its all my faults, talking about fight with the Apache's, I'm the blame for all that trouble. This my partner kept sayin—no fight, no fight. But I keep on saying fight, and we came near had a fight among our self.

Bitter Defeat

Chief Madzil say, Today I'm poor man, no more chief, as I lose all my mens. Though they put up a good fight They all died fighting. I should had listened to him, so we won't lose many of our men's, But I just had a bull head, that day, Chief Madzil says. When I got back home I spread the sad news. There Wailing among the Comanche people, They likely to killed him: This had been heard after they made peace with all the Lipan and Mescalero Apache, also No Water Lipan. Well after they made peace with the Mescalero Apache, old Madzil happened to be there too, after they settle up, Old Madzil got his name there.

Madzil they called him, Then he pulled up his buckskin jacket or shirt, and he show the scar on his body, You Apache have made all these scars; when we had a big fight at Coyote Mountain. (Which is now Davis Mountain.)

Yes said the Mescalero Men, you peoples should have let us alone that day and everything will be alright, but as you say, you wanted to be tough Comanche Chief,

Well said Madzil, From Now on we will be a good friend always,

Then Mescalero said. We have been looking for that long time, Since we are both Indian, and use only bow and arrow, Spear, and war club, We should not fight.

Then they begin to see the point, They said we fight with the Mexican and White if they make trouble with us, If they let us alone we too, be in peace with them,

Then said Mescalero, We can't do much now, since White Man got good firearm, It better to stay in peace, In the mean time, We make peace, so let's be brother and sister right along. They smoke some more friendship, They already said, Brother and sister to each other, Since then there no more trouble, They come to each other, when they happen to come to their country. They had a merry time together, horse race, shooting contest, and at night, They have friendship dance, They go raiding down to old Mexico together. All these things had happened many years ago, before my old Dad was born (about 1855). They visiting to each other to their country, but it hard time and lesson to learn for Madzil. So that the end of the story of Madzil.

Despite the desire for peace, and the smoking of the peace pipe among Comanche and Lipan, there continued to be problems. The desire to acquire horses and good stock was very difficult to overcome. Skirmishes and continual stealing of horses, killing warriors and then feeling bad about it, finding captive children and then settling down again until the next temptation caused much friction and conflict. Percy wrote other stories for his friends about hunting the wild horses, going out on raids and blaming the Comanches for everything.

At the end of one such long war story, Percy wrote:

But finally them mens had a big meeting, one day, When there came a big groups of Comanche, At the meeting Comanche men's stood up, and spoke, There are good many Comanche women too, In his speech the Chief said: Many time our men come down this way, and losing lot of them, So lets take peace smoke, So they did, Number time they did like that, But some of them don't let the Lipans horse's alone, The Chief says, It won't be that way from now on, This all happened *after* Chief Madzils trouble and we know how he blamed himself for many Comanche deaths and problems, Then they all happy. That night they had big friendship dance. They gave present to each other, all the troubles between them are settled, The Lipan Chief said, We don't bother you people, But the trouble is start from some of our own men, Lets be peaceable right along, and since then everything moving smoothly!

It's the end of my Comanche and Lipan story about their trouble. Hope you enjoyed it.

Unfortunately, the conflicts continued until both tribes were decimated and moved to various reservations. No longer could they have the free range of hunting, raiding and warfare. The end of the war trail had finally come but without honor or distinction and only in bitter defeat.

Chapter 15

APACHE VENGEANCE

Gold, Silver and a Pueblo's Demise

Courage above all things, is the first quality of a warrior.
—Carl von Clausewitz

Fue venganza, pura venganza…it was vengeance, just raw vengeance.
—rancher Francisco Fimbres, 1930

O ral tradition also preserved the details of a carefully planned attack on a small Mexican village in the Sierra Madre of Mexico, a major part of Apachería. Their homeland did not end at the border, and sometimes we forget that today. There were no borders with the Apaches, or at least not until the White Eyes created such borders and parameters on maps and in the minds of the settlers. These were points that both Daklugie and Percy, among others, made to Eve during their interview sessions. We have just learned about the great gathering in the Davis Mountains and the alliance with Juh's Nednhi or Blue Mountain Apaches and the Lipan/Mescalero group when fighting Comanches.

The storytellers especially enjoyed describing the events that unfolded after a very clever item—seldom used but still in the Apache war chest—was selected as a major blow to their enemies. It happened in Mexico. This version comes from a combination of Asa (Ace) Daklugie and Percy Bigmouth's recollections. Daklugie was actually present as a young boy when the victory celebration was made, and just prior to his death during the early winter months of 1955, he related to Eve what happened. Percy also repeated what

C.S. Fly's famous 1886 photo of four warriors, left to right, Yanosha, Chappo, Fun and Geronimo. We do not know why this brave man had such a name as Fun. We do know that the young warrior who threw the chile bomb into the crowded building from his position on top of the roof committed suicide in 1892 at about the age of twenty-six. He was a courageous fighter, and they say he saved Geronimo's life on several occasions. *Courtesy* True West.

he had learned over many years about this rescue, but he was born well after it had happened. By both men describing the raid to Eve Ball in the 1950s, we have preserved a dramatic account of an event few people on the outside knew had happened. Try to imagine if such stories had not been written down by concerned individuals like Eve or Percy. Eve, a historian, did this as a way to preserve a legacy of the people; Percy, the other individual involved, did so as a means to do the same, but not with the historian's eye to detail. This account is not written in the vernacular of the Apache but taken from a combination of interviews.

Warrior Fun's Strategy

They say that at one time, many women and children were captured and taken to Mexico. This time, it was not the Comanches but rather Mexicans who needed more captives to replace the ones who had died in the mines of the Sierra Madre. They say that our warriors plotted revenge for a major kidnapping of their women and children. The Apache warrior "Fun," a brave and very young man at the time, was the central figure in the rescue of families who had been made into slaves, working long hours in Mexican silver mines.

So, this is how the rescue happened long ago in the land of the hated Mexican enemy. It is the story of how a chile grenade created chaos and rescued imprisoned Apaches.

Geronimo's *segundo* and half brother, the warrior known as "Fun," climbed stealthily to the earthen roof of the *iglesia*. The Mexican standing guard had already been killed silently with a knife by Martine, one of the bravest of Apache men. The others—mostly Chiricahua, and a couple Mescalero, Lipan and Bedonkahe—waited in the darkness until all the community of despised miners gathered in a small adobe or what you call church.

Geronimo gave details:

When the "medicine man" (*Padre*) made lights in the big room, we watched him kneeling at the feet of his God. He then arose, went to a rope, and the pulling on that rope sent out loud noises. People began coming. We lay hidden until we made sure that everybody in the pueblo had entered. Heavy logs and rocks barricaded the entrances. Now came the most important part of their daring plan for which any mistake meant death to the captive women and children. They waited silently, desperately, until Fun's work was completed.

Fun was very clever. He ground hot chile pods, added *ocote* [flammable pine pitch] and he carry it in [a?] heavy buckskin shirt. Using fire sticks he light *ocote*, let it smolder a moment and then dropped it into the barricaded building from a hole he had dug earlier. Covering the opening with a blanket he move back into the shadows. The poorly lit interior and the crowded miners panicked. Mexicans try to break their way out of smoky church. Their coughing loud, and they were crazy to escape. The chile smoke grenade [much like tear gas that we would use today to control crowds or create chaos with pepper spray] kept giving off poison and choking, burning smoke and penetrating chile smell that destroy nose and eyes.[21]

As confusion everywhere, the Apaches quietly and very quick kill all guards by the adobe where their families are prisoners. They also steal supplies and ammunition including thick leather bags of gold and silver already packed for the mule pack train trip to Chihuahua City. They go through the houses of the Mexican miners taking what they needed.

There were some very young boys and the Apache took them to raise as warriors—not to keep as slaves.

Heading back to Juh's stronghold at the top of the zig-zag trail near Blue Mountain, there was much relief. Though they lost two valiant men, they knew that a great celebration would occur because of this day.

This was a rescue like no other. It was not "hit and run," as were most of their strikes, but the strategy put into place had required observation, planning and timing. And no Mexicans dared to follow them into their lair at the top of the Blue Mountain. Skeletal remains at the bottom of the trail were proof that no one could breach the stronghold because Juh had his watchful guards cast planted boulders upon them or rain down arrows, killing any survivors. Their bleached and broken bones and saddles remained as examples to all comers. Old Scout Bigmouth had gone many times with his adopted family into Mexico and was familiar with many of these places.

After weeks of searching, the Apaches had finally located the captives, who had brutally been kidnapped while out gathering *mescal*. Anger and revenge filled their hearts. When scouts brought word that the women and children were working in the mines lugging loads of ore and rock, *venganza* (vengeance) was the only thought in their hearts. The Apache found a way to communicate that help was to come, soon, and that they must not starve themselves. Facing slavery was worse than death, so the women were simply refusing to eat. But now the captives had hope.

No man can stand to see his women and children crowded into corrals or sent off as slaves or to fates even worse than death. No warrior people would accept this terrible scenario. The Apache were no different. They had numerous weapons within their war chest, and in desperate circumstances, they used one of the most clever of these contents in this daring raid.

A Pueblo's Destruction

This is what happened that day. The old-time elders said afterward that big rock and earth slides totally destroyed the hated *pueblo* and, along with it, the proof of their big rescue. When asked, the Apache did not know the name of the *pueblo*, only that it no longer existed.

Destroying the *pueblo* of the hated Mexican mining community was sweet revenge. Above all else, the Apache held great disdain for these miners because they grubbed in the bowels of Mother Earth for the yellow and silver iron. Gold was sacred to their god, *Ussen*. It was unacceptable to use except in dire times. However, these were dire times, and gold, like silver, could be used to purchase ammunition, guns and food. Old Nana and other leaders had indicated it was acceptable to use gold dust or nuggets.

Perhaps Nana explained it best. He was ancient, but he was tough. He held out his wrinkled hands, with silver in one. "Silver," he said, "is acceptable to use."

In the other he held gold. He said:

> *This yellow earth is sacred to our people and to* Ussen. *It is permissible for us to pick up nuggets from the surface, but not to dig in the earth like the miners. If we do so, the great Mountain God spirits will shake their mighty shoulders and they will destroy us and everything. We all appreciate life,*

Nana fought well into his eighties, dying at Fort Sill as a POW.

however to the White Eye, it is his greed for gold that he values more. It is not good. Gold will cause our people to lose their land, and their lives. Now it has value for us to purchase guns and supplies, but in the end we will also be destroyed by the greed of White Eyes and Mexicans.[22]

The Apache always had ways of exacting cruel revenge, and this rescue would become part of the folklore and colorful mosaic of the land we call *Apachería*. If it had not been for a few who survived the raid and their ancient oral history tradition, the account could have been lost forever. Old

Nana was asked to relate the story that night around the campfire and especially at that first celebratory occasion. Nana was a great storyteller, and he would have enjoyed describing for the rest of the war-weary people in Juh's stronghold the bravery of Fun, Kaytennae and Martine. However, he declined and asked Geronimo to describe the raid. Geronimo did so in detail, and that is what we have repeated here by Apaches who had these words repeated to them over time.

Though they lost two in the daring rescue, the women and children's shining and happy faces that night were reward enough. And thus this raid became part of the Apache legends and lore of the Southwest.

This photo of Ace Daklugie at Mescalero Ceremonial grounds was taken in 1939, sixty years after the raid. He was a young boy of twelve or thirteen during the telling of this story, after the victorious warriors returned. Geronimo was his uncle.

Chapter 16

CONCLUSION

Crossing Over the Bridge

To look upon that landscape in the early morning, with the sun at your back, is to lose the sense of proportion. Your imagination comes to life, and this, you think, is where Creation was begun.
—Scott Momaday

The Earth does not belong to us…We belong to the earth.
—Chief Seattle

Living in the shadow of the Sacred Mountain for so long had tempered Father Albert's life. He loved the mountain, he loved the people and he is buried inside St. Joseph Mission to the right side of the altar. The Sacred Mountain had also become his coveted haven, in life and in his passing on to the land of *Ussen.*

Father Albert, the brown-robed Franciscan, had begun his mission work among the Apaches and was often seen riding horseback or driving his buggy at a fast pace to visit various family bands scattered throughout the huge Mescalero reservation. By now he was a revered and recognized figure. He knew most of the families: the Shantas, the Daklugies and Chihuahuas; the Bigmouths; Enjadys, Cochise and Naiches; the Magooshes, Comanches, Kanseahs and Gaines; Seconds, Palmers and Kaywayklas; and many others. He had grown to admire them all and in turn had been accepted into their family gatherings. Father Al did not make harsh judgments, and even those

The Sacred Mountain, Sierra Blanca. *Photo by Mary Serna.*

Apaches who were not Catholic greatly admired him, welcoming him into their homes. In this way, he also learned additional details about the life and beliefs of the people.

He had described for Eve the first time he saw the Sacred Mountain from the Three Rivers side. He was going to visit the Shantas, a prominent family living at Three Rivers. He and Father Ferdinand left early one morning, and though dark when they departed the mission, upon leaving Tularosa, they saw the brilliant sun burst above the brooding and towering Sierra Blanca, and it truly took their breath away. It was a magnificent scene with the mountain on one side and the shimmering white sands desert to the south. It was clear that Sierra Blanca, the Sacred Mountain, claimed the horizon and would continue to do so for centuries to come.

Ferdinand's purpose was to introduce Father Al to that part of the Mescalero reservation. He noticed that Father Albert was totally enchanted with this view of Sierra Blanca, so he decided to tell him the legend about the mountain as he had come to understand it. This was before Father Al came to know the legend so well himself.

194

Three Rivers Chapel with Sierra Blanca in the background. *Photo by Mary Serna.*

The mountain was their point of origin on this earth. What Father Ferdinand told the Franciscan was similar to versions that Eve had recounted so many times to various friends, but his version was much shorter.

In those days, everything lived on Sierra Blanca, and all the creatures and plants spoke the same language. *Ussen* asked them to go out and choose any spot they wished as their home. The spruce, the aspen and firs all selected the high, cold country. Humans and the ponderosa pines decided to go along the streams and rivers. Juniper and cedars went below the pines. Then all living things came down the mountain, leaving trails that eventually eroded into arroyos and canyons. Some creatures decided to live in the streams, although, as Father Albert found out, most Apaches of that era did not eat the trout or other water creatures. Everyone lived in peace, and it was a good life at the base of the Sacred Mountain.

It was a beautiful and simple story, one that the young priest never forgot. Later, Percy told him a similar but much longer version confirming how reverent the Apaches were and how they seemed to be so much more at peace in their world than the white man was in his.

Father Albert had arrived at Mescalero in 1916. He baptized and gave communion to many who had gone for years without this ceremony that was

Father Albert as a young man just arrived at Mescalero. *Courtesy Saint Joseph Apache Mission.*

so important to the Church and the people of the isolated parish. During the next two years, he began planning to build the St. Joseph Church. In January 1918, Percy Bigmouth was confirmed, and a friendship began between the Bigmouth family and Father Al. He had much to learn, and he could not have better teachers. Twenty-five years later, he would meet Eve Ball, and they, too, would become close friends.

Everything comes in circles, so they say, and thus it was that he introduced Eve to old Scout Bigmouth and Percy. And the rest is history.

During an interview session with Scout Bigmouth, Percy told Eve more about their beliefs and legends and about the influence of the "brown robes" like Father Albert.

Eve noted that it was indeed a beautiful story.

Percy replied that it *was* a beautiful story—and true.

It was a fortunate writer who was permitted to listen to Percy, "Old Dad" and many other tribal elders. And now, through the books by Eve Ball and the pages written by Percy and sent to Gene Neyland Harris and Mary Montgomery, we have been allowed inside part of the world of Apache legends and lore. Although we do not have Percy speaking out loud, we have his handwritten pages, and we know he wrote as he spoke. Furthermore, Eve, Gene, Mary and others have helped to "iron them out good."

Perhaps by reading these touching and humorous stories, we can now better understand the life, legends and cultural traditions of a people often vastly different from our own. Hopefully we can also say after savoring every line and every lesson, "Job well done and *mil gracias!*"

The bridge has been constructed. It is now up to each of us, in our own special way, to cross to the other side.

We are lonesome animals. We spend all of our life trying to be less lonesome. One of our ancient methods is to tell a story begging the listener to say and to feel, "Yes, that is the way it is, or at least that is the way I feel it." You're not as alone as you thought.
—John Steinbeck

Notes

Part I

1. Read general information in Almer N. Blazer (edited by A.R. Pruit), *Santana: War Chief of the Mescalero Apache* (Taos, NM: Dog Soldier Press, 1999). For additional good sources regarding tribal history see Lynda A. Sánchez, *Fort Stanton, An Illustrated History: Legacy of Honor, Tradition of Healing* (Ruidoso, NM: Write Designs, 2009; second edition, 2010) and Martha L. Henderson, "Sacred Sites Sustaining Tribal Economies: The Mescalero Apache," (PhD diss., Evergreen State College, November 2007).
2. Terrell, *Apache Chronicle*, 340.
3. Ball, *In the Days of Victorio*, xiii.
4. Ibid.
5. Inn of the Mountain Gods website, http://innofthemountaingods.com, is another good source for contemporary materials.
6. Eve Ball, interviews from 1975 to 1982.
7. Sinclair, "Bigmouth's Father Remembered Happy Days, Before 'God-Damns' Came to Dirty Water."
8. Interviews, Eve Ball; Haley, *Apaches: A History*, 240. General Carleton was probably the only man in the Southwest who wanted a reservation at Bosque Redondo. He stubbornly insisted, and no one countered his wish, so they established the hated "concentration camp." After it was built, one of the soldiers at the fort wrote about what a terrible place it

was, mirroring the Bigmouth account. "The Rio Pecos is a little stream winding through an immense plain, and the water is terrible, and it is all that can be had within 50 miles, it is full of alkali [*sic*], and operates on a person like castor oil—the water, heat it a little, and the more you wash yourself with common soap the dirtier you will get."

9. Poem published in the *Carrizozo Outlook*, August 22, 1913. The document was forwarded to the author by Karen Mills, historic records clerk, Lincoln County, New Mexico.

10. Information courtesy Allan Radbourne. In 1883 and 1885, we see notations for Bigmouth being on the rolls for six months at a time. I have not checked all rolls, but his name is clearly there during those years. Corroborative evidence proving that Scout Bigmouth served is found on the extracts from *Register of Enlistments...Indian Scouts*, vol. 153 (N.A. Microfilm Publication M233, roll 71, record group 94).

11. Haley, *Apaches: A History*, xi.

12. Eve Ball, interviews, many, 1975–82.

13. Lynda A. Sánchez, "They Loved Billy the Kid, To Them He Was Billito," *True West*, 1984.

14. The vast majority of material came from Eve Ball interviews and letters written to Gene and Mary, and they have been noted as to date and source. All materials are in author's files.

Part II

15. S.M. Barrett, ed., *Geronimo, His Own Story* (New York: Ballentine Books, 1970): 61–64, 179–80.

16. Ibid., 179–80.

17. From interviews with Mack Bigmouth, June 1979, and Eve Ball, 1975–1982. Similar bat tales are common to all Apache bands.

18. Ibid.

Part III

19. The excerpt selected comes from *Native American Testimony: A Chronicle of Indian-White Relations from Prophecy to the Present, 1492–2000*, edited by Peter Nabokov, no date available but this edited version of Percy's story has been repeated in many sources over the years.

20. This material about the Apache/Comanche battles came from Percy's written accounts on the now famed Big Chief tablets. Today, everyone

recognizes that this account, based on what his father and mother related, is rare indeed because few Native Americans wrote down what they heard from tribal elders.

21. In the country of India today, the local military and police forces are using one of their native chile pod products, the hottest in the world, for crowd control and also in rural villages for protection on outer barricades from wild foraging elephants. "'The chili grenade has been found fit for use after trials in Indian defense laboratories, a fact confirmed by scientists at the Defense Research and Development Organization,' Col. R. Kalia, a defense spokesman in the northeastern state of Assam, told The Associated Press. 'This is definitely going to be an effective nontoxic weapon because its pungent smell can choke terrorists and force them out of their hide-outs,' R.B. Srivastava, the director of the Life Sciences Department at the New Delhi headquarters of the DRDO, said. Srivastava, who led a defense research laboratory in Assam, said trials are also on to produce bhut jolokia–based aerosol sprays to be used by women against attackers and for the police to control and disperse mobs." From the Huffingtonpost.com (2010) or Google the topic, as there are many articles and videos about this *new* weapon. However, it is not really *new*, as we have seen in this tale from the Sierra Madre.

22. Quotes and the account in general come from interviews with Percy Bigmouth and Daklugie as told to Eve Ball, 1954–55.

BIBLIOGRAPHY

Books

There are an incredible number of sources and books about Apaches. In addition to these below, I would recommend checking out the bibliography in each or simply Googling the topic.

Ball, Eve. *In the Days of Victorio.* Tucson: University of Arizona Press, 1970.
———. *Ma'am Jones of the Pecos.* Tucson: University of Arizona Press, 1969.
Ball, Eve, Nora Henn and Lynda A. Sánchez. *Indeh, An Apache Odyssey.* Norman: University of Oklahoma Press, 1988.
Barrett, S.M., ed. *Geronimo, His Own Story: The Autobiography of a Great Patriot Warrior.* New York: Ballentine Books, 1970.
Blazer, Almer N. *Santana: War Chief of the Mescaleros.* Taos, NM: Dog Soldier Press, 1999.
Boyer, Ruth M., and Narcissus Duffy Gayton. *Apache Mothers and Daughters.* Norman: University of Oklahoma Press, 1992.
Cave, Dorothy. *God's Warrior.* Santa Fe, NM: Sunstone Press, 2012.
Dobie, J. Frank. *Apache Gold and Yaqui Silver.* Albuquerque: University of New Mexico Press, 1928, 1967.
Emerson, Dorothy. *Among the Mescalero Apaches: The Story of Father Albert Braun, O.F.M.* Tucson: University of Arizona Press, 1973.
Greene, Jerome A. *Fort Davis National Historic Site/Texas (Historic Resource Study).* N.p.: National Park Service Publications, U.S. Department of the Interior, 1986.

Haley, James L. *Apaches, A History and Culture Portrait*. New York: Doubleday, 1981.

Leckie, William, with Shirley Leckie. *The Buffalo Soldiers: A Narrative of the Black Cavalry in the West*. Norman: University of Oklahoma Press, 2003.

Naylor, Thomas, and Charles Polzer. *The Presidio and Militia on the Northern Frontier of New Spain*. Vol 1. Tucson: University of Arizona Press, 1986.

Sánchez, Lynda A. *Eve Ball, Woman Among Men*. Ruidoso, NM: Write Publications (Lincoln County Historical Society), 2007.

———. *Fort Stanton, An Illustrated History: Legacy of Honor, Tradition of Healing*. Ruidoso, NM: Write Publications, 2009; revised, 2010.

Sonnichsen, Dr. Leland. *The Mescalero Apaches*. Norman: University of Oklahoma Press, 1966.

Terrell, John Upton. *Apache Chronicle*. New York: Thomas Y. Crowell Company, 1874.

Thrapp, Dan L. *The Conquest of Apachería*. Norman: University of Oklahoma Press, 1967.

Internet Sites

www.civilwarcavalry.com

www.fscsp.org

www.innofthemountaingods.com

www.musketoon.com

Magazines and Newspapers

Alamogordo Daily News

El Paso Times

Gadsden Times. "Last Apache Dies at 108" (Scout Bigmouth obituary), December 2, 1958.

McGraw, Kate. "A Tribal Feeling." *New Mexico Magazine* (January 1980): 32–33.

Ruidoso Free Press

Ruidoso News

Sinclair, Al F. "Bigmouth's Father Remembered Happy Days, Before 'God Damns' Came to Dirty Water." *Southwesterner* (May 1963): 10.

Smithsonian Magazine, November 2013.

Zimmerman, P.G. "The Little Bonito, Child of the Snow." *Carrizozo Outlook*, August 22, 1913. Courtesy historic records clerk Karen Mills, Lincoln County Archives, New Mexico.

General Repositories Containing Items Related to Percy Bigmouth

Brigham Young University (Eve Ball Papers)
University of New Mexico, Center for Southwest Research, Albuquerque, New Mexico
University of Texas at El Paso Library, Eve Ball Collection, 1887–1976, MS 117, C.L. Sonnichsen Special Collections Department
University of Virginia, Southwest Collections

Correspondence

Harris, Dr. Jackson, letters, April 14, 1981; May 14, 1981; October 12, 1987
Montgomery, Mary (Spencer), numerous e-mails, 2012, 2013
Radbourne, Allan, e-mail, March 28, 2006
Serna, Mary, numerous e-mails, visits and interviews, 2009–2014

Oral History Interviews

Ball, Eve, many from 1975 to 1982
Bigmouth, Mack, June 1980
Chee, Ralph, Eve Ball home, summer 1978
Darrow, Ruey, Eve Ball home, 1979–80
Garcia, Filadelfio (Phil), numerous interviews from 1975 to 1980, Lincoln, NM
Garcia, Juan, several interviews from 1775 to 1981, Lincoln, NM
Harris, Gene Neyland, 1984, 1985 (two by phone)
Henderson, Danna, daughter of Dan Kucianovich, several e-mails and personal visits from 2007 to 2014
Herrera, Santiago (Jimmy), 1980, my home

Hinton, Dr. Harwood P., from 1978 to 1984

Klinekole, Virginia Shanta, her ranch home at Three Rivers, 1984

Leyba, Tony, interviews from 1974 to 1976, Lincoln, NM

Montgomery, Mary, e-mails from 2012 to 2014 and personal visit/interview, June 24, 2013

Naiche, Amelia, granddaughter of Cochise and daughter of Chief Naiche, Mescalero (1979) with Eve Ball

Naiche, Mark, Eve Ball home, 1978, 1979

Sánchez, Altagracia, many interviews, San Patricio, NM

Sánchez, J. Jaime, many interviews, Lincoln, NM

Sánchez, Mauro, interviews, 1978, Mauro Sánchez home, Hondo, NM

Second, Bernard, Medicine Man, Eve Ball home, several interviews, 1980

Serna, Mary, several interviews and many discussions from 2000 to 2014

Zamora, Cristóbal, several interviews, 1981, his home, Lincoln, NM

Zamora, Fulgencia (Mama Z), interviews from 1979 and 1980, her home, Lincoln, NM

Other

Gene Neyland Harris obituary. www.Harpeth Hills.com, October 29, 2009.

Henderson, Dr. Martha L. "Sacred Sites Sustaining Tribal Economies: The Mescalero Apache." Evergreen State College, Louisiana, written on behalf of the Mescalero Apaches.

Register of Enlistments…Indian Scouts, Volume 153, (N.A. Microfilm Publication M233, Roll 71–Record Group 94), courtesy Allan Radbourne.

WPA Writer's Project. Interviews by Edith Crawford, 1930s.

About the Author

L ynda A. Sánchez, author/historian and retired educator, has called historic Lincoln County, New Mexico, her home for more than four decades. Variety is the "essence of her life, as well as the spice." Her time serving in the Peace Corps (South America) and her archaeological field work adventures in Mesa Verde (Colorado), Sonora, Mexico and for the Blue Creek Maya Research Project in Belize have provided part of that variety. New Mexico author Eve Ball was her writing mentor, and all of these experiences greatly influenced and guided her to the colorful mosaic representing folk heroes, legends and the incredible history of the Southwest. Being an advocate for historic preservation caused

Author at Fort Stanton. *Photo by Joseph Arcure.*

her to devote a decade to the preservation of historic Fort Stanton, including writing a book on the topic, *Fort Stanton, An Illustrated History: Legacy of Honor, Tradition of Healing.* Her other books include *Eve Ball, Woman Among Men*; *Indeh, An Apache Odyssey* (co-authored with Eve Ball and Nora Henn); and *Capture the Past for New Mexico's Future* (co-authored with Linda Hart and Karl Laumbach).

Lynda is a member of Western Writers of America and the New Mexico Archaeological Council. She freelances for *Arizona Highways*, *New Mexico Magazine* and *True West* and has written over 250 articles for various publications and newspapers about her passion: history of the Southwest and historic preservation. She notes, "It is incumbent upon us as a nation to preserve our heritage for future generations. A society that does not respect its heritage has no future."

She has served on the Bureau of Land Management Resource Advisory Council and the Lincoln County Historical Society Board of Directors (as both vice-president and president) and was vice-president of the Fort Stanton Development Commission. She taught teacher workshops using the science of archaeology as the means to inspire youngsters in math, science, language arts and biology. She also obtained a National Park Service grant for an archaeological survey of the Fort Stanton lands. She speaks before numerous groups and is an advocate for our veterans' legacies. Lynda is the recipient of many awards related to these fields, including a "cavalry sword" for work on preserving Fort Stanton and *True West*'s 2007 Best Preservation Project in the Nation award. The Historical Society of New Mexico also honored her in 2008 with the L. Bradford Prince Award for her preservation work.

At present, she serves as a member of the Fort Stanton Cave Study Project Board of Directors, a science-based 501c3 mission that is surveying and exploring the world-class Fort Stanton Cave. She is the project's public outreach liaison. Another special activity takes her to the Mescalero Apache homeland, where she is a volunteer at St. Joseph Apache Mission and Veterans' Memorial. This is where she met Mary Serna, who is one of her "preservation heroes."

Lynda and her husband, James (retired educator from the New Mexico Military Institute), raise *corriente* roping cattle and live along the beautiful Bonito River in Billy the Kid country. They have one daughter, Katherine, who is employed by the United States Forest Service.

CPSIA information can be obtained
at www.ICGtesting.com
Printed in the USA
BVHW03*2242050618
518277BV00006B/19/P